TELL
ME,
RABBI

Morris N. Kertzer

TELL ME, RABBI

Bloch Publishing Company
New York

Acknowledgments

Many friends and associates have made this book possible. I am grateful for the editorial assistance of Roberta Dunn, who lavished so many hours of sacrificial devotion upon this manuscript. I am especially appreciative of the encouragement given to me by Rabbi Albert Plotkin and Sam Levenson, whose incomparable sense of humor and wisdom impelled me to seek a wider audience in print for the stories which I have shared with them.

Most of all, the real inspiration for this book came from the heart and mind of one person, my wife Julia, whose patient, persistent and perceptive comments added a new dimension to *Tell Me, Rabbi.*

*I had originally planned to dedicate this book
to Ellen, Sharon, Daniel, Joshua, Seth and Molly,
who call their grandfather, Zaida.
But, nine-year-old Daniel suggested: "Why not
dedicate it
To all who are made in the image of God?"*

The heart has a longer memory than the mind.
That is why a story clings more tenaciously to us than a
statistic.
How much more so if the story happens to be true.
A wise rabbi in ancient Israel once said:
"Never under-estimate the value of even a simple story,
For it leads us to God's truth.
A king may lose gold or a precious jewel,
And it often takes no more than a penny candle
To find it."

Contents

Introduction:
"Tell Me, Rabbi"

How does it feel to go through all your adult life with an extra label prefixed to your name?

For those outside the orbit of synagogue life, the word, rabbi, does not fall lightly from the lips. Numberless times, I am greeted with the double question: "What shall I call you? Rabbi?" The music that accompanies the second question calls for a note at least an octave higher in the last syllable, reflecting tentativeness, amazement, disbelief and a kind of amusement: "Really? Do people really call you *that?*"

The title, rabbi, is redolent of archeology: a character jumping out of a biblical page, or an ancient scroll. Why not call you Prophet Goldstein, or Patriarch Silverman, or High Priest Finkel? Even Roman Catholic priests do not call themselves, Priest—.

The only people I have met, beyond the circle of Jewish religious life, who speak the title with ease, were employees of a race-track. When they ask one another, "Who's your rabbi?" they are inquiring of their fellow job-holder: "What politician got you your job?"

Rabbis share with clergymen of other faiths a feeling that they are regarded as not exactly a normal species of human being. Every banquet speaker reminds them of their disembodied status when he begins: "Ladies and gentlemen, and reverend clergy. . . ." a third sex!

I walk into the Recreation Room of our Club, and a player at the pool table whistles: "Hey, fellows, here comes the rabbi. Watch the language." On occasion, the transition to respectability may be somewhat gradual: "Cool it, guys, the rabbi. . . . Cut out the (expletive deleted)"

In a social gathering, when I am introduced, the air of normalcy evaporates. "Oh, you're a rabbi . . .

"I haven't been to services for over a year."

"That reminds me, I have to pay my Welfare Fund pledge."

More frequently, the first words that greet me are:

"Do you know *our* rabbi: He (select one of the following:)

(a) is the world's worst preacher.

(b) is a regular guy. His golf handicap is seven.

(c) is hanging on to his job with his teeth.

(d) has a beautiful wife.

(e) has a crummy wife.

(f) is a terrific business man.

Then, inevitably, the Saturday night gathering degenerates into a discussion of Temple problems, rivalries, finances, Sisterhood politics or the struggle to keep their children within the fold. The rabbi's plea, "I'm not working tonight," falls on deaf ears.

At a summer resort, or on the beach, there is no escape. Even a bathing suit is no disguise. "Rabbi, I've been waiting for months to talk to you. Tell me, rabbi, what can I do about my son's future in-laws. . . ." I once escaped to the anonymity of a Miami Beach motel, and stretched out in the Florida sunshine, at pool-side. It had been a long seven-day-a-week year. Within five minutes, the motel owner approached and introduced his friend.

"Tell me, rabbi, would you mind helping out a friend

of mine? He came home from his New York office last Monday, and found a note on the kitchen table. His wife had left him and the children. He came down here to Miami to recover from the shock."

Symbolism plays a large role in the life of a clergyman. In a sense, he is a walking symbol, in or out of "uniform". For many people, the mere presence of a "man of God" conveys a message. I walked into the hospital room of a beautiful young woman. When she caught sight of me at the threshold of the door, she cried out: "My God, it's true! I'm going to die!"

Her suspicion that she had leukemia was confirmed the last week of her life by the sight of a rabbi.

I have been ambivalent about the necessity of wearing a distinctive garb. A number of Protestant clergymen have recently begun to emulate their High Church colleagues. Perhaps it is the better part of wisdom to signal your profession, for instant identification. It sometimes rescues us from embarrassing situations.

Uniform or not, once my identity as a rabbi is revealed, many hazards grow out of that discovery.

"You don't look like a rabbi!"

Variations on that theme include:

Complimentary: (on a plane to New Orleans) "I thought, at first, that you were a dress manufacturer."

(A gushing Texas matron:) "You, a rabbi? You're much too nice to be a rabbi!"

Wonderment: (On a Boston-New York train A priest, sitting next to me, learns that I, too, had been an army chaplain:) "That means you are a rabbi. I couldn't tell from your accent!"

Uncertainty: (A ninth-grade student) "Tell me, rabbi, what do you do for a living?"

Our profession calls for being in earnest most, if not all, of the time. This book is largely about the importance of not being too earnest about ourselves. One of the following vignettes delineates the image of a rabbi which young children envisage. A child's artlessness and his capacity for candor instills in his rabbi—or in any clergyman—a much-needed humility. Some of the vignettes are about people who take themselves too seriously. Others suggest that, even if our life-work consists of moral preachment to others, it is good to cultivate a gift of humor about ourselves. Humor and humility are two sides of the same coin.

My ideal rabbi, in this respect, was the late Rabbi Morris Adler of Detroit, Michigan. His first love was scholarship. He told me, in our student days, that he planned to devote his career to academic pursuits. But his remarkable oratorical gifts, in more than one language, his love of people, and his inordinate passion for creating a just society, brought him into the active ministry. Morris Adler's tragic end, on Lincoln's Birthday, 1966, on the pulpit of his Detroit synagogue, was a reflection of his entire life. Toward the close of a Saturday morning service, in the presence of well over a thousand worshippers, including two hundred visiting Catholic nuns, a demented young man leaped to the altar, gun in hand, and demanded that the wrongs of the world be righted.

The rabbi had counselled the youthful member of his congregation, and realized that he might become violent. Morris Adler pushed aside others on the altar, to keep them out of firing range, and tried to placate the weapon-wielder. Two shots were fired, fatally wounding both the rabbi and the young man. Close to 20,000 mourners gathered, early in March, (the rabbi lingered, unconscious, for a few weeks) to pay tribute at his funeral.

Morris Adler's last words, in an eloquent sermon, were: "May the love that Lincoln had, even for his enemies, the wisdom with which he embraced every situation be ours." Then, he suffered Lincoln's fate.

Rabbi Adler could abide anything but pomposity and pretentiousness. He once passed a Temple, of cathedral-like proportions, in a city he was visiting. On an impulse, he walked into the Temple office and sought an appointment with the rabbi. With much difficulty, he was allowed to meet the rabbi's secretary who was visibly annoyed at the stranger's expectation that he could see the eminent rabbi without prior appointment.

The man Morris Adler wanted to see was a prolific writer, extremely egotistical about his talents, especially about his books, although they were singularly lacking in both content and style. The secretary spoke sharply to the Detroit intruder:

"You definitely cannot see the rabbi now. He is busy writing a book!"

With an impish smile, Morris Adler replied:

"Oh, that's all right. I'll wait!"

* * *

The following stories, all based on fact, and, with only a change in names for obvious reasons, are a modest attempt to capture a little of Morris Adler's spirit. Had he lived, he would have suffered torment about the present state of humanity. Life, in these 1970's, is serious: life is earnest. Only serious and earnest answers to its problems should engage us. But, as Sholom Aleichem would say: In the meantime, a sense of humor is essential to those who would lead the way, lest they lose that sense of perspective that is indispensable to redemption.

Childhood in the Frozen North

I was sixty years old before I put together the pieces of my early childhood.

These words are being written on October 18th, 1974, in the Valley of the Sun—in Scottsdale, Arizona. Temperature this afternoon: 97 degrees. My first memories of an October 18th, my birthday, are of a world bounded on one side by railroad tracks, running right in front of our log-cabin home in Northern Canada. Our "backyard" consisted of a vast forest of spruce, birch and poplar trees reaching out endlessly—to the trackless uninhabited world of Hudson Bay country. By October's end, snow had covered the ground for several weeks. Eighty miles *south* of Cochrane, my birthplace, was a sign which read: "Arctic Watershed. From this point North, all rivers flow into the Arctic."

Other memories. Sitting in a school room on my fourth birthday. All eight grades sat in the forty seats of the school. In front of each of the eight rows was a Union Jack-Maple Leaf flag, which was lowered only when there was a vacant seat in that row. Even when the weather hovered near 55 below zero, you came to class, because your absence would mean a lowered flag, and disgrace to your Grade.

School at four? I was an unregistered enrollee. That

October, I had annoyed the teacher by following my older sister and brother to school, and, when she caught a glimpse of me shivering in the cold, she brought in the human snowman to thaw out near the potbellied stove in mid-classroom.

Still another memory: Fire. Flames were a constant companion of fear in the summer bush-country. In my pre-school years, we went through three major forest fires, driving us to the safety of the South. I thought I remembered peering through the windows of a train carrying the fire refugees, our heads covered with soaking wet towels as protection against the smoke. Last year, I told my father's Cochrane companion, now ninety years old, about that recollection. He corrected only one detail. It was not a passenger car. The town kept a number of freight cars on a siding near our home, and we were huddled into open gravel cars!

The Kertzer general store, the only two-story building in town in 1913—we lived upstairs—was spared in the Big Fire of that year, because a group of gold prospectors manned a vigorous bucket-brigade. They had a stake in our store. Father's safe contained their gold, entrusted to David Kertzer because they were in the bush country much of the year.

Our last fire—the one which drove us south to Toronto—hit our home directly. We children were rescued in a mattress slung over the husky shoulder of Grischa, a young Russian who lived with us as a helper in both our store and home. We learned to talk to him in his native tongue. We sang scores of Slavic songs and developed a basic peasant vocabulary that was more Ukrainian than Russian.

The trauma of fire involved a personal encounter when I approached my third birthday. My father's Hebrew diary contains the following item: "My son, Morris, was burned on August 6th, 1913, and remained in serious condition for over three months." That day, I had tried to imitate the lumber-jacks whose customary manner of lighting a match was to strike it against the seat of their pants. I was enveloped in flames and the family ran to Dr. Henderson's office across the way. The doctor, who had brought me into the world, was the only physician within a hundred miles, and had been engaged by the T. and N.O. Railroad Company.

When healing began, he removed a layer of skin from my thigh, and sewed it on my under-arm. Surgeons, who have seen the results many decades later, have marvelled at the skill of a country doctor. They find it hard to believe that the surgery was performed without a nurse, with no anesthetist to administer the chloroform, the doctor's instrument, my father's razor. My ninety year old friend added one detail I had never known before: the whole surgical procedure took place on the kitchen table of our log-cabin.

It was not until I was sixty that I retraced the steps of my parents, to learn about their early married life in the bush country of Northern Ontario. From interviews with oldtimers, some in Cochrane, others in San Francisco and New Jersey, and from the back-files of the Cochrane Northland Post, I discovered that the year of my birth coincided with the birth of Cochrane as a town. I was the first non-Indian born in the frontier community.

My father, David, had come as an immigrant in 1907, leaving my mother, Pearl, and their two children in Russia. Together with two companions, natives of the same village, he worked on the railroad which was being built by the Temiskaming and Northern Ontario Company, thrusting a "needle of steel" through one of the most impenetrable forests in the world. During the brief non-snow period of the year, heavy rains would wash away a month's labor. Bridges collapsed and disappeared. Some of the workmen were actually driven out of their minds by the enormous black flies which attacked them for weeks on end. Every pound of material to build the tracks had to be carried on the backs of laborers. There were no roads. Massive loads were transported by six-oar freighter canoes on dangerous rivers, or by dog-sled. (I asked an old aunt of mine how she managed to visit us from her home in Iroquois Falls. She unblinkingly answered: "By dog-sled and canoe! How else?")

All my life, I have marvelled at the hardihood of my parents in settling in the bleak wilds of that sub-Arctic world. What were my mother's thoughts when she arrived, a year before I was born, to find that her new home in "the golden land of America" was a flimsy cabin of logs, reinforced with tar paper, to shield them from the 50 below zero winds of a December blizzard? What was it like to have wolves and bears for neighbors? To discover that her only source of water was melted snow? To wait till June for Lake Commando to melt so that she could bring pails to its shores?

To overcome loneliness, we would travel to Porquis Junction or Matheson or Kirkland Lake where our relatives had settled. There were railway tracks to those settlements, but the trains ran only three times a week, and it was more convenient to use a railway handcar. "Keeping kosher" entailed a complicated procedure: the meat was placed on a locomotive cowcatcher in North Bay, hundreds of miles to the south, and was picked up as it came into the railway yards near our home.

David Kertzer's motives in coming to the bush country were told to his children in our childhood. He believed that Jews should not emigrate to urban centers.

They should be pioneers, like his Odessa cousins who had settled in Palestine in 1879 to help build up the country. Soon after my father landed in New York, he read that the Canadian north country was opening up, and 160 acres of land were being offered free to homesteaders. He and his two companions took up the offer, only to learn that rights to the land were contingent on cultivating a tenth of it within a certain time. When I visited Cochrane, whose population of 4,700 was 300 less than it was in my childhood, I realized that very few of the adventurous pioneers could possibly clear the immense woods. Early accounts tell of elephants being borrowed from a visiting circus to make a clearing large enough for a performance.

The Kertzer family finally compromised: they opened up a general store. Mother would join her husband in trips to Indian communities, and canned goods were exchanged for fur pelts. Some of their more enterprising neighbors sought out the riches of the area, and came upon vast fields of gold, silver, copper and cobalt. Others exploited the inexhaustible store of lumber. In far-off New York City, trucks on Broadway proclaimed that the paper on which their news was printed originated in our northland community.

But the Kertzer family was content to expand its modest general store. They had little time for exploration. My earliest childhood memories are of a constant stream of relatives, mother's and father's, joining us in the north country, all brought into Canada by the sacrificial efforts of my parents. The first words I remember reading were on the envelopes of letters that came with Russian stamps, using the address that the European relatives found on the upper-left hand corner of our store stationery:

Mr. and Mrs. D. Kertzer
You Can Save Money By Buying From
Geller and Kertzer
Cochrane, Ontario, Canada

No trace of the Kertzer clan remains in Cochrane. A history of the town, written to commemorate its golden anniversary, records that after the Big Fire of 1913, when only the Kertzer store remained standing, that "much to their credit Geller and Kertzer refused to raise their prices . . ." The writer of the article also describes the first play ever produced in the Northland. In the summer of 1915, an all-female production was staged, entitled, "Ladies Aid of 1860." The cast included Mrs. Pearl Kertzer. I imagine that with mother's limited command of English, she was probably in the dance line.

The only reference to me was in the June 10, 1915 issue of the Northland Post. Cochrane's Public School announced its promotion list for the year. After reporting the marks of all the pupils from 8th to 1st grade, the bottom line offered this mysterious reference to their only four-year old student:

"Promoted from Class E to Class C: M. Kertzer." I can't remember that.

David and Pearl Kertzer realized their early dreams as pioneers. When the radio brought "The Maple Leaf Forever" into our living-room, Dad Kertzer would stand glued to attention, and his eyes filled with a kind of mist that spoke of pogroms in Russia and freedom here. When he reverently mentioned Prime Minister William Lyon Mackenzie King, he expected us to be over-awed by the mere cadence of his name.

I don't think of those days very often. When I was graduated from college, at nineteen, I moved permanently to the United States. But occasionally, something of David Kertzer's spirit is kindled in me. A television program carried the voice of Alistair Cooke, in accents redolent of my youthful days, described the death of King Edward VII, "and there came to the throne of the British Empire his son, King—George—the Fifth." That was my *first* King. A lump stuck in my throat all evening, and, long after the 11 o'clock news, it was still there.

"Love Thy Neighbor" Can Be Very Exhausting

Our national tradition, reinforced by the prodding of all our religious groups, has elevated Brotherhood as second only to Motherhood on the scale of sanctity. Each year, during the week of St. Valentine's Day, we indulge in an orgy of "love thy neighbor", called Brotherhood Week. It is the season of the year, at the lowest ebb of winter, when Protestants, Roman Catholics and Jews declare: "I love you, you love me; we are all one happy family."

In days past, when life was more personal and less structured, a community would organize Brotherhood rallies; arrange exchange of pulpits; or build some programs around the theme of "love thy neighbor". Clergymen would travel in teams, a Catholic priest, a Protestant minister, and a rabbi, to preach the Brotherhood of Man. Newspaper editorials would pay tribute to the trio, and feature photographs of their sympathetic faces—as a dramatic symbol of mutual respect and tolerance. The word tolerance, a popular poster-word in the first decade, later fell into disrepute. It was too patronizing, and was jettisoned in favor of "good will". Even that phrase had to be discarded: it had overtones of hypocrisy.

As a matter of fact, the vocabulary of benevolence has a very short life-span in our culture. A preacher of love is always one step behind the contemporary dictionary. He urges his congregants to do good—and the do-gooder falls from grace. He exalts the virtues of compromise and appeasement (what a beautiful word, "appeasement".) in a world of tension and conflict, only to discover their respectability gone. He encourages his members to express their concern for underprivileged youth by becoming active in a big-brother movement, but the shadow of "Big Brother" looms dark on the horizon. I am beginning to suspect that the reason the ambitious programs of the '30's and '40's went out of style is that they ran out of words.

A Brotherhood team, in which I participated, appeared before a packed auditorium in Clinton, Iowa. After our performance, an elderly lady rushed up to the stage to greet me.

"Rabbi," she gushed, "I'm not of your faith, but I sure appreciate your loud voice. My ears have gone bad, and I didn't hear a word of those two Christian gentlemen. Why do our Christian preachers always mumble? I don't care too much about your religion, but you rabbis sure come through loud and strong."

Each of the trio was equipped with an arsenal of brotherhood stories. Under the umbrella of good-will, we were permitted to twit our fellow panelists with jokes about their faith. There was an ever-present danger of skating on the thin ice of sectarian sensitivity. A Protestant spokesman, who lived in a small Illinois community on the bank of the Mississippi, described an episode in his Methodist church. Only two Jewish families lived in his town, and, for want of a synagogue, their children attended his Sunday School. Both the Strausses and the Rothschilds had seven-year-old children. During Easter Week, only the Rothschild youngster was present when the teacher presented the story of the Crucifixion. When she heard the words, The Jews crucified Jesus, the Roth-schild girl reacted. "M . . . m . . . m . . . Couldn't have been us. It must have been the Strausses."

More innocuously, we made humorous references to the Baptists and Methodists as temperance bugs; Cathol-ics thought that Heaven was a branch office of their Church. Jews wouldn't take off their hats in their Church. One of my Catholic fellow-panelists was carried away on the subject of Jews as the finest people in the world.

"Just look at all the stores on Main Street. What signs do you see? Levinsky's Furniture Store. Kaufman's Men's Wear. Cohen's Hardware. Finkelstein's Super-market. They own every last store on the block. That's the kind of Jewish citizens we have in our town!"

The cleric reminded me of a eulogy I heard in a small Southern city. The deceased, a porter in one of the cam-pus buildings, was an upright church member, accord-ing to his preacher.

"There are some who say that Sam liked his whiskey too much. I don't believe a word of it. Some folks said that Sam had sticky fingers. I've never known Sam to touch anything that didn't belong to him. As for those stories about Sam and the ladies—why Sam was a fine, God-fearing Christian."

One problem, in ecumenical adventures, was to gauge the sophistication of our audience. Many a denomina-tionally monolithic community knew little about other faiths. When I taught at the University of Alabama, I would receive mail addressed to "Catholic Chaplain", University of Alabama." I brought a package to the post-master in order to catch the expression of amusement on his face when he read it.

"What's wrong with that, rabbi?"

"Just listen to what you're saying. Rabbi—Catholic

Chaplain." He thought for a moment.

"I guess you're right. I keep getting the two of you mixed up."

In the mid-thirties, I attended an inter-faith rally launched by the local Roman Catholic priest to protest Mexican persecution of the Church.

"Morris," Father R. pleaded, "you know that every time they persecute the Jews, I'm the first to stand up and be counted. You heard my speech against Hitler."

At the community meeting, the speaker, representing youth, denounced the evils of fascism. The Presbyterian spokesman dwelt broadly on the need for combatting bigotry. Except for the Chairman, I was the only speaker who made reference to Mexico. On the following morning, in a front page picture, the Chicago Tribune depicted me, finger pointing skyward, over the caption, "Rabbi Denounces Mexican Persecution." I studiously stayed clear of that country for over three decades.

Rabbis generally establish a bond of affection with their Christian counterparts. In a secular age of religion embattled, we have to huddle together for warmth. A rabbi becomes a confidante of a Christian colleague, who pours out his heart about his problems with the laity. Such confidences are less likely to get back to the church. And there is often the natural fellowship of kindred spirits. In the army, the Episcopalian chaplain would complain to me about some of the Southern "hell and damnation" preachers. "The trouble with those fellows is that they don't realize that you can be Christian *and* comfortable at the same time." For a number of reasons that sociologists and psychologists may explain, Jewish and Episcopalian clergyman often find themselves on the same wave-length.

There is a built-in paradox in the very nature of organized religion. To preach and teach love, compassion, mercy, altruism, loving kindness, and at the same time, to declare that the only path to love, compassion, etc. is through the instrument of *our* church or synagogue creates a monumental kind of contradiction. Love and truth somehow seem to get into each other's way. For if you insist that yours is the path of salvation, how can you avoid convincing your new pew-holders that "there is no salvation outside . . . ?"

Over the years, I have received a thousand letters—every time my picture is in a newspaper or on a television screen—from men and women who have found the truth and wish to share it with me. (Oddly enough, as these words were written, a letter arrived simply addressed to "The Ruling Rabbis of Scottsdale, Arizona." The message, emblazoned in red ink, contained the warning, "Who so despiseth the WORD shall be *destroyed.*" (Proverbs 13.13) The number alone strikes fear. I was doubly annoyed. First, because some one was quoting *my* King Solomon against me. Secondly, because our post-office never delivers any letter which does not have every last detail correct, and here they go beyond and above the call of duty to place, at my doorstep, a letter without either a name or an address on it.)

Hardly a week passes that I do not receive a message in the mail from some one who cannot endure the thought that I have forfeited my seat in Paradise. My conception of Hell is a heavenly abode peopled with all those letter-writers.

What acute insight Dr. Bonaro Overstreet has given me in understanding the psychological mechanism which lies behind many church and synagogue people! I have read her essay, "The Unloving Personality and the Religion of Love," almost as often as I have the Book of Genesis. Especially these words: ". . . the church (she could add, "the synagogue") attracts to itself in conspicuous numbers certain types of unfulfilled, unloving personalities—particularly those who live by imitating love . . . they become "pillars" and "watchdogs". . . . Hence a paradox: the internal policy of a church dedicated to the religion of love is often largely determined by those who are basically unloving."

Psychologist Overstreet does not limit her observation to those who sit in pews. "No one can say how many who are in the Christian ministry are there because they love mankind and how many are there *because they do not love mankind.* (Italics, hers.) Of course, she could have included all faiths.

She would probably be disturbed by the annual reports of church affiliation which reveal that those religious bodies, which concentrate on universal brotherhood, either remain static in numbers or regress. Some of the historic universalist churches have not grown in a century. On the other hand, the "why can't people be like us?" churches experience annual increments greater than the total membership of the "liberal" churches.

As I look back on over a thousand appearances before church audiences, I detect little variation in the pattern of the question-answer period. Whether the study group is High Episcopalian, Lutheran, Latter-Day Saints, Roman Catholic or Pentecostal, certain questions persistently come to the fore. Even when the parking lot of the church is crowded with Cadillacs and Lincolns, one parishioner will always ask: "Rabbi, why is it that so many Jews are rich?"

How does one answer the question, "Why don't you folks accept Jesus?" I have wrestled with that one for forty years, and each year I find myself answering in a different way. My current reply is: "My religion is the Mother Faith. You don't ask the mother why she doesn't follow her daughter's beliefs. Isn't it more natural to ask why the daughter doesn't follow her mother's religion?" It is the kind of retort which satisfies the speaker more than it does the audience.

The most lethal question usually comes from a benign-looking old lady, a placid smile permanently etched on her face, assured that life has already supplied her with all the crucial answers. After a recent Church Sunday School class presentation, one such matron rose to offer a comment, attached to which she latched a booby-trap question.

"Fifty years ago, in Ohio, we had a visiting missionary speaker in our church. He was a converted Jew preaching the Gospel. He told us that, when he embraced Jesus, his Jewish family beat him unmercifully. He still bore the scars. Now, my question, rabbi. . . . (her smile took on a glistening radiance) is this: Do you folks still do that to your children?"

Almost a quarter of a century of my professional career has been devoted to inter-religious work. At one point in my career, when I was serving in a Temple pulpit, I was invited to return to inter-faith endeavor. I shared my conflicting feelings with a colleague who had spent a lifetime in ecumenical labors.

"Sol, isn't it a hard enough job trying to make Jews into better Jews? Why should I take on the extra burden of attempting to make better Christians out of Christians?"

He answered, in the classic style of the rabbis, with a parable, a rather modern one.

"There were two sextons in a small town in Russia, both serving small synagogues. One sexton asked his friend how much he earned and received the reply, "twenty-five rubles."

"Twenty-five rubles! How can you live on that?"

"Oh, my job is very easy. I have only one duty to

perform. Every morning, I climb to the synagogue roof and look to see if the Messiah is coming. If I see him riding down the street on his white horse, I'm supposed to rush down and summon the Head of the synagogue."

"But only twenty-five rubles a month?"

"I know it's not much of a job, but, at least, it's a lifetime proposition."

"Love thy neighbor" is an exhausting lifetime proposition, but so is every other kind of love.

Battling for a Name

"Our baby is going to be a girl!"

"What makes you so sure," I asked her.

She looked toward her young husband who sat at the edge of the sofa in my study, and caught his reassuring glance.

"Robert and I just know that it's going to be a girl. It *has* to be!"

"Which is it—it's going to be—or it has to be?"

"Both. I'm just beginning my seventh month, but we'd like to have your help, rabbi, in choosing a name."

For the next hour we went through the familiar routine of discussing the various traditions in Judaism about baby-naming. Sephardic Jews, those from the Mediterranean Basin, have few restrictions. They often use the name of a living grandparent. But Ashkenazic Jews, which include most of European Jewry, follow the custom of naming a newborn child after a deceased relative. (Many American Jewish parents seem to have abandoned the tradition. One year during the early '70's our Temple Bar Mitzvah rolls included 23 Stevens and 19 Jeffreys, all 1958 babies.)

The couple's problem of selecting a name had grown to United Nations proportions. Who were the authorities in such matters? Aunt Sadie, whose credentials consisted in once having spoken to a rabbi in Brooklyn; great-uncle Joe, vice-president of his Temple's Men's Club, and cousin Saul, who had just retired as Commander of the Jewish War Veterans' Post in Newark.

Commander Saul reminded them that Sharon's late uncle's name, Solomon, could not be memorialized because this name was too close to his own. Aunt Sadie insisted that all that Jewish tradition demanded was the use of the first letter. Abraham could readily be transmuted into Alden. Joe was only interested in perpetuating the memory of Grandma Rifka, his sister.

A month after the initial counselling session, Sharon and Robert returned for further inquiry. By now I suspected that they were desperate to have the baby at the Cedars of Lebanon Hospital in California. But their minds were still unyielding. It was going to be a girl. It just had to be a girl!

At seven, one morning, the phone call came. Robert's voice quivered with the news, "It's a boy!"

He implored me to come to the hospital as soon as I could. Disaster was in his voice.

The emergency meeting took place in the maternity wing, with four in attendance: Sharon, Robert, his mother, and myself. The day-old baby slept a few yards away in the Nursery.

Mrs. Blum, the new grandmother, launched the attack.

"When my Henry died, may his soul rest in peace, I couldn't wait for him to have a namesake. Henry was a wonderful husband, such a wonderful father, and, I don't need to tell you," (grasping her son's knee) "a great provider. He built up a big business out of nothing, and our Robert fell into a gold-mine when he dropped out of college. Right, Robert?"

Her son turned up his palms in helpless acquiescence.

Sharon lifted the bed covers as if ready to jump out of bed.

"Mother, you know how I feel about the name, Henry." Her voice grew hoarse as she turned to me.

"Rabbi, I just can't stand the name Henry. When I was sixteen I went steady with a boy named Henry for over a year. He was really a loser, a creep. I just can't live with a baby named Henry."

I thought I had a perfect solution to the dilemma. In fact, more than one formula for pacifying both contenders. Plan 1. As a rabbinic authority, I reminded Mrs. Blum that only the Hebrew name mattered. "Henry's Jewish name was "Hirsch", I believe. Let's give him that name at the Circumcision, and you can call him anything beginning with "H". Aunt Sadie told you that."

Mrs. Blum, Sr. gave me an "enemy camp" look. Plan 2 added little oil to the waters.

"Not only can you give him the Hebrew name, Hirsch, but you can have his English name, Hirsch or Hershel. Don't forget, Mrs. Blum, Henry's authentic name, religiously speaking, was Hirsch."

The baby's mother was ready to compromise, although she wasn't too happy with an old-fashioned appellation. But Mama had resumed her chant: "After all Henry did for his boy!"

A nurse entered the room with the birth-certificate application, and she left, leaving one line with the words: Baby-boy Blum.

A week later, Sharon called me from her parents' house.

"I came home to my folks, rabbi. Robert has moved back with his mother. The folks would love to have you come over and see our Christopher."

Fiddler On the Balcony

My wife was born and reared in the city of St. Catharines, in Southern Ontario. St. Catharines is known as the Garden City of Canada, not more than a dozen miles from Niagara Falls. In the days of our courtship, I visited there frequently. The small Jewish community had built an attractive synagogue, which was the scene of quite a number of Gretna Green type of weddings. An American, living in Buffalo, only thirty-five miles away, would call the Canadian rabbi, who happened to be the closest one to the border, and explain that his fiancée was an alien visitor, She could only regularize her status as a permanent resident by a marriage outside the borders of the United States.

One Sunday afternoon, my father-in-law-to-be, the perennial president of the congregation, received a distress call from his rabbi.

"We are here in the *Shul* (synagogue)—we have a Buffalo wedding, and we are four men short of a *minyan*. (the quorum of ten men needed for an Orthodox wedding ceremony) "Will you come over, Mr. Hoffman, with your sons? Maybe your future son-in-law is in town? We may need him, too."

I joined the family for the ceremony. The groom appeared to be in his middle thirties, diminutive, with a harried look suggestive of a decision made in haste and with considerable reservations. The bride towered over him in both height and weight. And she had a few years advantage over him as well. When she smiled, one had the feeling that she had left her dentist in Warsaw before he had time to finish her denture work.

The ritual of witnessing the documents was accomplished rather laboriously, as the rabbi was meticulous in recording all the Hebrew names. We squirmed impatiently for the wedding rites to begin. With only a handful of guests, the ceremony was certainly going to be informal.

We were mistaken. The bride insisted on leaving the sanctuary, so that she could make a proper entrance, and march down the aisle in dignified fashion. The groom and his parents took their places under the canopy, and the rabbi's wife moved toward the entrance, to escort the bridal party into the sanctuary. The bride took one step —and halted.

"What's wrong? Why doesn't she come in?"

The buxom bride whispered her complaint to the rabbi's wife who ran forward and delivered the message to her husband.

"She won't budge without music!"

"What music? Where can we find music?" An Orthodox synagogue does not permit use of an organ, and, in any case, where would one locate a musician at a moment's notice?"

One of the local residents reminded the rabbi that Lapidus, the tailor, played the fiddle. The indefatigable rabbi's wife flew downstairs to the social hall, and we heard a nickel drop into the pay phone.

"Lapidus, please come to the *Shul* quick. And bring your fiddle."

We were reconciled to the loss of our Sunday afternoon, and we waited for the fiddler to arrive. Lapidus, dishevelled and out of breath, reported to the rabbi.

Where would he stand? The bride intimated that it would be most romantic if Lapidus went upstairs to the women's balcony, and sent out his dulcet tones over the bridal party. Now, the procession was in order, and all the principals in place.

As the bride took her first step into the sanctuary, we heard the wobbly notes of the opening bars of *The Volga Boatman*. U—U—UKH—*NYI!*—the measured cadence of the tired oarsmen on the Russian river. U—U—UKH—*NYI!*

"Lapidus!" we motioned to the fiddler in the balcony. "Play something else! How about a wedding march? For heaven's sake, Lapidus, play anything else!"

"I don't know anything else", lamented the musician on high. He continued playing, "U—U—UKH—*NYI!*"

The bride was totally oblivious to the commotion. Without breaking her stride, she marched with studied pace, and with a radiant smile that lent an aura of comeliness to her happy face.

An ancient Talmudic law requires wedding guests to greet the groom with laudatory comments about the bride's loveliness. What about the commandment about bearing false witness? "That is no problem", declared the gallant Talmudic rabbis. "Every woman, on her way to the marriage canopy, is beautiful!"

Bar Mitzvah Blues

When LIFE magazine was in its prime, I received a visit from one of its editors. He was planning to do a piece under the rubric, *LIFE Goes To a Bar Mitzvah*. At the time, the popular journal was running a series on the great religious shrines of the world, and I naively assumed that the Bar Mitzvah story would fit into that series. But, as our conversation progressed, I realized that the editor had something else in mind. He was eager to include our Bar Mitzvah service in the long-running *LIFE Goes To a Party* series. The focus of his interest was in opulence, not observance. I told the editor that we were not interested in his project.

A few months later, LIFE ran a *LIFE Goes To a Bar Mitzvah Party* story. A thirteen year old Philadelphia boy was depicted, attired in an expensive tuxedo, swallowing two pheno-barbital pills in preparation for the Bar Mitzvah ordeal. Covering half a page of LIFE was a photograph of the young man standing beside his elaborate gifts, including a hi-fi set, a typewriter, and a television set. On the other side of the mound of presents stood two Pinkerton detectives, retained to protect the treasure-trove.

In a sense, the LIFE editors were reporting fairly. There are Bar Mitzvah celebrations like the Philadelphia extravaganza. But they are far from typical, and many sensitive Jews cringe when they are portrayed in novels and movies, such as *Marjorie Morningstar* and *Good-Bye, Columbus.*

Most Bar Mitzvah (Bat Mitzvah for girls) ceremonies demand years of preparation for the youngster. Aside from mastering the unfamiliar Hebrew, the thirteen-year-old child must learn a very exacting ancient chant and, most difficult of all, is required to stand before hundreds of friends and strangers to "perform".

A rabbi's function, in these circumstances, is not only that of teacher and mentor. He is often called on to cope with the boy's nervousness. Twice, while addressing the Bar Mitzvah boy, I have felt his head fall on my shoulder in a brief fainting spell. Standing at attention, his eyes glued on the rabbi's face, the boy may be mesmerized and suffer a Buckingham Palace guard syndrome.

One boy, I recall, trembled at the thought that he would forget his lines. He was certain he would collapse midway. A few minutes before the hour of decision, as he was about to be summoned, our sanctuary began to fill with smoke. The boy's face lit up in happy expectation: deliverance was at hand. I debated whether we should halt the service, but nodded to the boy to proceed. We had heard the distant sound of fire-engines, but did not associate it with our problem. As Marvin rose from his seat, firemen, fireaxes on their shoulders, burst into the sanctuary and ordered us out of the building. Marvin's prayers had been answered!

The firemen spent over forty minutes, using heavy blowers to clear the air of smoke from a recalcitrant oil burner.

We filed back in. The fire-fighters had not only expelled the smoke. They had managed to exorcise Marvin's anxieties, and he rose to a flawless chanting of the

Torah and the Lesson from the Prophets.

Some rabbis are so offended by the circus quality which occasionally marks the celebration part of the Jewish *rite de passage*, that they seriously consider abandoning the Bar Mitzvah practice. After all, it has no roots in the Bible or in ancient tradition. And even more dismaying is the tendency of the children to drop out of Religious School right after the big event, which makes the Bar Mitzvah a kind of terminal disease.

In the English-speaking world, the United States, Canada and Great Britain, the lavish Bar Mitzvah seems to stimulate the imagination of some parents, aided and abetted by caterers and even florists. There is, for example, the thematic Bar Mitzvah.

I refer, of course, not to the synagogue service, but to the festivities following the religious event, most often on Saturday night. A thematic Bar Mitzvah centers on a specific motif. Father or son may be lovers of golf or football, perhaps sailing. Each table is accordingly decorated to resemble a golf green or a football. At one such celebration, on Long Island, the guests had to walk a gang-plank to gain entrance into the hall.

One such theme was carried to the very entrance of a Westchester sanctuary. As the guests left the Temple on their way to the Country Club banquet, they were greeted at the foot of the entrance by two gaily decorated horses drawing a carriage. At the reins was the father, who had slipped out moments before the Benediction, and now, fittingly costumed, shouted, "On to Camelot!"

Sometimes the caterer and the florist, inspired by Las Vegas, conspire to emulate some of its ornate settings. One such caterer proudly reported to me his greatest achievement. In the midst of the Bar Mitzvah dinner, the lights were lowered and a spotlight focussed on a flower-bedecked chandelier near the ceiling. To the accompani-

ment of the percussion section of the band, the chandelier slowly moved lower. The huge flower parted—and
out stepped the five-year-old sister of the Bar Mitzvah
boy, wearing a diadem of flowers on her head upon
which were glued thirteen lit candles!

In less affluent communities, the thematic Bar Mitzvah may be more modest in design, but no less imagina-
tive. At a Brooklyn celebration, the highlight of the dinner was a dramatic sketch, staged by the Cantor. On a
raised platform, the presiding Cantor had arranged a
Succah, the traditional tabernacle ordinarily seen only on
the Feast of Harvest. Above the tabernacle hung a bright
marriage Canopy, a *Chuppah.* The Bar Mitzvah boy
stepped on to the platform, and, from within the hut rose
the Cantor's voice. "Who goes there?"

The Bar Mitzvah boy called out, "I, Samuel, the son
of Joseph."

"What is your desire?"

"I wish to enter the Household of Israel."

"What is the password?"

"Shema Yisroel—Hear O Israel, the Lord our God is
One."

"You may enter."

Rabbis of today contend with problems unknown to
their predecessors. In my earlier years, I seldom had to
deal with a Bar Mitzvah boy whose parents were di-
vorced. Today's youngsters, with four parents, present
untold problems. Who accompanies him to the altar, the
step-father with whom he has developed excellent rap-
port, or the natural father long removed from the scene
and two years behind in support payments? What if the
natural father is not even invited, and threatens the rabbi
that he will disrupt the ceremonies if he summons the
step-father to the altar?

Ironically, the broken home is not necessarily an occasion for tribulation. This is the conversation I overheard at Bar Mitzvah class:

"You fellows are lucky. You've got four parents! Ronnie cleaned up at his Bar Mitzvah last Saturday. One of his grandfathers gave him a movie camera and when another grandfather heard about it, he gave Ronnie a ten-speed English bike. He's sure that he'll be getting a tape recorder and a hi-fi set from the other two grandfathers. And you never saw so many aunts and uncles and great-aunts and great-uncles. Some Bar Mitzvah! Me, I've only got two parents."

Act of Faith

No point of involvement in the lives of other human beings, for the rabbi—or minister or priest—compares with his contact at the moment of marriage. When he officiates, at either end of life, or even during rites of passage, such as Confirmation or Bar Mitzvah, the clergyman is more or less a witness, in a psychological sense, a bystander. His prayers and blessings effect no fundamental change in the status of those whom he touches. But, in presiding over a wedding, he is intimately engaged in *changing* the very identity of two human beings. Even the State recognizes this fact by designating him an instrument of government.

I have often been asked whether I became bored after the thousandth wedding ceremony which I performed. How can any sensitive person not be emotionally affected by the opportunity to share in the moment when two young people commit a tremendous act of faith, by selecting the one person, of all the people on earth, with whom they intend to spend the rest of their lives? I must admit that some of that magic has been dimmed by my awareness that "forever" is not as long a time as it used to be. Perhaps one bride out of a hundred will say to me, in our pre-marital conference, "if this doesn't work, I'll try again."

Each year, my batting average has gone down: ten years ago, over 95 per cent of my weddings stood the test of time; today, it is closer to eighty-five per cent. As the casualties mount in the marital arena, a rabbi takes even more seriously his responsibilities in insisting upon pre-marital meetings with the couple. On at least three occasions, I have bowed out of a ceremony by telling the prospective bride and groom that I refused to be an accessory to the crime. A medical student made reference to his fiancee's plain looks, but wryly observed that her family's wealth would come in handy in launching his career. I suggested that they find another rabbi.

A clergyman cannot play God, but there have been times when one of the bridal couple terminated the engagement after our three-way encounter. I asked the boy and girl, sitting on my study sofa, what they had in common. The prospective groom, in his late twenties, responded crisply, "Nothing." He seemed to mean it. Only four days remained before the wedding. His fiancée burst into tears, picked up my telephone and asked her mother to inform the 225 invited guests that there would be no wedding.

Later, I learned that our interview was the climax of other crises. The previous Sunday night, she had waited, in vain, for her fiancé to appear at the end of her bridal shower, so that she could proudly introduce him to her friends. After midnight, the frantic girl had driven to a town in the neighboring county, and, as she passed the home of the young man's ex-girl friend, she discovered his car. He was bidding a last farewell. A year later, I officiated at her marriage to a more durable groom.

Playing the role of mediator, in pre-wedding skirmishes, sometimes brought me into eye-ball to eye-ball confrontation with one or more of the parents. A tearful bride-to-be sought my assistance in placating her mother in Arkansas who refused to grant her blessing to the match. Nor would the mother release any of the girl's trust fund which her late husband had set up for the marriage of his daughters. I met with the Arkansas matron, and warned her that she was jeopardizing her relationship with her daughter, but the mother was adamant. She did not plan to attend the wedding, and explained her negative attitude:

"When Rosabelle's father died, seven years ago, on the day of the funeral, I had my daughters make a solemn promise that they would only marry a millionaire. My older girls have honored the promise that they made over their dear father's grave. But, not Rosabelle. She is marrying a lawyer!"

I launched into a defense of the young man's family, whom I knew well. He was the son of a prominent attorney; his mother was a well-known scientist. Her future son-in-law, at the age of twenty-seven, was associated with a reputable law firm. The bride's mother was unimpressed.

"But, he's a lawyer!"

"Why is that so bad?"

"Why, he's no better than a doctor. If one of them gets a heart attack, his income stops then and there. But, a business man, like my late husband—he still draws an income."

The compromise that I negotiated was not too mollifying. The mother of the bride attended the wedding, held in the home of the groom's parents. During the rites, to express her disappointment in the only daughter who had dishonored her father's memory, the matron remained aloof and huddled in a corner of the living room.

Some mothers begrudge the spotlight in which their daughters bask, and conspire to share in the limelight. I officiated at a lavish hotel wedding in the grand ballroom of a Chicago hotel whose seating arrangement provided a center aisle about half the length of a football field. When I arrived, I noticed a microphone hanging from the nuptial canopy, and assumed that it was placed there to amplify my voice for the large gathering. I discovered that the instrument had been set up for the cantors,— three cantors, who were brothers—who were well-known in the city. These gentlemen, wearing white satin robes, trimmed with gold, marched down the aisle. Before the bridal procession, they circled the microphone, their lips less than an inch from it, and sang, "Because." Not just one or two verses of "Because", but at least six. I imagine that they must have written the words of the last three verses.

In addition to a seemingly endless procession of bridesmaids, the bride's immediate attendant was her mother, also dressed as a bride! She explained that today was her twenty-fifth wedding anniversary, and that this ceremony was to be followed by a re-run of her own. I indicated that I would have to defer to the three cantors, and that I would take a seat after I had blessed the young couple.

From my seat, in the rear of the ballroom, I watched the two brides march back to the end of the aisle and reverse roles by exchanging veils and corsages. During the interlude, the triple cantors offered the guests a brilliant rendition of Rimsky-Korsakoff's "Flight of the Bumble-Bee," in close harmony.

The wedding ceremony took ninety minutes. The marriage lasted six months.

The nuptial drama is heightened by the tremendous investment of all the principals. Every rabbi has witnessed a number of faintings—best men, bridesmaids, and, at times, even the bride or groom. One of my colleagues, in Northern New York, fainted while he was officiating.

A number of Reform rabbis follow the custom of pausing during the middle of the Service, and inviting all those present to share in a few moments of silent prayer. I am not positive about the genesis of that custom, but a colleague of mine confessed that he was probably the originator. Many years ago, in the middle of a ceremony, he realized that he had neglected to bring the marriage certificate to the altar. After a moment of panic, the rabbi bade the principals and guests to bow their heads for a few moments of silent prayer for the couple. Hastily, he retreated to his study, and retrieved the necessary document. At the conclusion of the ceremony, several of the guests told the rabbi that the highlight of the Service was the beautiful moment of silence. He not only incorporated the dramatic pause into his standard ritual, but recommended it to his fellow-rabbis.

The most *involved* wedding participant I have ever met was not even a relative. He was an English professor in whose department the bride was a graduate student. The girl's parents were unable to attend, but had sent their blessings. Their place was taken by the professor, an effervescent, middle-aged bachelor who bounced rather than walked. He brought the bride to the scene of the wedding, and also furnished the food and drinks for the repast.

As the ceremony began, he sat down at the piano and played the accompaniment as he sang, "O Promise Me." Then followed a lively rendition of the wedding march, (the professor was an organist in his church), after which he leaped to the entrance, escorted the bride down the aisle, and gave her away. During the entire procedure, his tears flowed freely. His weeping was renewed when he waved farewell to the couple. They drove away on their wedding trip in *his* automobile.

On the same campus, during my early years as a rabbi, a marriage of two graduate students produced a crisis I have faced only once. A few minutes before the start of the ceremony, as I was coaching the groom on his part in the Service, which included only nine Hebrew words and the "I do," he opened his mouth, and not a word emerged. We assumed that he was suffering from laryngitis, and the best man drove to a drug-store for a throat spray. Medication did not help. His face was contorted as he mouthed the words, "I do," but not a trace of sound came out of his mouth! A psychologist friend took me aside, and speculated that his friend was probably suffering from "hysterical aphonia," a loss of voice brought on, at least subconsciously, by misgivings.

I recalled that ancient law provided for the marriage of deaf-mutes by means of sign language, but I was uncertain if it applied in the present situation. Happily, in less than an hour, the young man was able to whisper the required eleven words. So far as I know, the speechless groom and his bride are still married.

One of my older colleagues, who has officiated at weddings for well over sixty years, confided to me that he had never followed the practice of pre-marital interviews. He was well aware of the complications generated by family problems. For him, a rabbi's function was to officiate, not to referee.

Since I have not benefitted by his wisdom, I have been designated as a mediator in countless disputes. Who marches down the aisle and in what order? What are the rules about the kind of music that is appropriate? The theme song from "Love Story"? (popular for a number of years, even though the story itself involves a tragic ending) How about "The Second Time Around", when the occasion calls for it? Are any of these less fitting than the traditional Mendelssohn, (a renegade from the Jewish faith) and Wagner (a Jew-hater)? What happens when the bride's family invites 150 guests, and the groom's side is limited to ten?

A couple appeared in my study for a small wedding.

Accompanying them were two over-sized dogs. The groom pointed to them:

"Rabbi, you suggested that I use my close friends as witnesses. These are my closest friends."

"What kind of dogs are they?"

"German shepherd."

"Religious law requires that they be Jewish."

The groom was unconvinced, but, over his protests, the dog witnesses were removed.

That was a few years ago. As the winds of custom have shifted, I have relented a little. On two occasions, at garden weddings, the family dog has trotted down the aisle, and, strangely enough, those present took the matter in stride. In one case, the canine bridesmaid was bedecked in the same be-ribboned color scheme to match the other four bridesmaids.

It is futile to argue with parents planning a wedding that there is no such thing as standard processional procedure, hallowed by centuries of tradition. I have shown them encyclopedia articles under the heading, "Marriage", with photographs of scenes in Warsaw, Paris, London and Bucharest synagogues. The parents are certain that the Brooklyn style, that they have seen for the past twenty-five years, follows an example set by Father Abraham when the biblical Isaac and Rebecca were married.

During the Second World War, in Marseille, France, I officiated jointly with a French rabbi in the wedding of an American officer and a local bride. As we entered the sanctuary, Rabbi Salzer quietly indicated to me that this was a *troisième classe* affair. How did he know it was a "third-class" wedding? By the color of the canopy. Maroon, signified third class. Blue, was the motif for second class; white, for first class. The difference, related to the Temple fee schedule, was in the floral decorations, the number of potted palms, and the size of the choir. Our *troisième classe* service entitled the family to one soloist and two potted palms. One Gallic touch was the lighting: only half the Synagogue lights were lit.

As the music began, the bride and her entourage entered. Then, a special flourish of the organ ushered in the central figure of the day, the groom. Following the benediction, the bride and groom left in a horse-drawn carriage, the same means of travel used by her Provençal grandparents and their grandparents.

One significant change in wedding patterns grows out of the increasing number of second and third marriages. Over a period of years, like many clergymen, I have performed the wedding of a girl in her late twenties; many years later, I have been called on to preside over the funeral rites of her husband; and, with the passage of time, she has invited me to bless her marriage to a second husband.

In the days of my youth, my widowed aunts and great-aunts prided themselves in their widowed status. In the 1970's, marriages for couples in their seventies is a frequent occurrence. One groom, at seventy-six, was escorted by his grandson, who served as best man. The old gentleman's hearing was impaired, and, in the middle of the blessing, he swept his sixty-nine-year-old bride into his arms, and kissed her. His grandson separated the couple, and whispered to me that time was precious to the old man.

Time has not diminished the sense of excitement I feel when a couple stand before me to exchange their vows. The years have only sharpened my awareness of life's uncertainties. The Talmud declared, almost two thousand years ago, that "marriage is like a ship setting out on the high seas. Most return safely."

A June bride and groom came to my study in September of 1956. They asked me to fill out a duplicate of their wedding certificate. What had happened to the original? After a honeymoon in Europe, they had returned on the *Andrea Doria*. As the Italian liner neared the coast of Newfoundland, it was struck by the Swedish ship, the *Stockholm*, and the honeymoon couple found themselves on a life-boat with all their belongings lost. Would I replace the document that was somewhere afloat in the North Atlantic?

The last words of my nuptial benediction are: "May you be blessed with length of years, and vigor of mind and body." Often, I think, as I repeat the blessing, of the "Andrea Doria", and the two young people floating among icebergs off the Newfoundland coast.

'Twas the Night Before Yom Kippur

I sometimes wonder if the rabbi of my youth would have been able to reach the modern congregant, child of an urbane culture, the typical worldly sophisticate. Even on Yom Kippur, that solemn day of repentance when, according to tradition, the Divine Judge determines "who shall live and who shall die, who at the full measure of his years, and who not at the full measure," the average congregant is not particularly moved to "fear and trembling", I try to imagine what would happen if Rabbi Gordon of the '20's were to belt out one of his fiery Yom Kippur sermons.

The gray-bearded rabbi would cast his eyes upward, gazing not heavenward, but toward the woman worshippers who sat, ancient fashion, high up in a semi-circular balcony. He would shake his forefinger as his arm swept from one end of the gallery to the other.

"*Meine teiere yiden*—my beloved Jews, for every face I see before me, I behold a monument with a name on it. One name for every face, on that monument." His words would trigger a loud sustained wail from the gallery worshippers, including my mother and her sisters, and, as his finger seemed to count off the faces, one by one, the chorus of lamentations rose to a crescendo that sent shivers down to the male worshippers below. When the rabbi cried, "repent!", we repented.

A colleague of mine, in recent years, had a different impact on his Yom Kippur eve worshippers. His eloquence was no less fiery. He, too, summoned the faithful to penitence.

"Yom Kippur is a time for examining our souls, for checking our lives. Why can't we treat our souls as seriously and as vigilantly as we treat our automobiles? All this month, we will be bringing in our cars for the Fall checkup. We'll make good and sure that the oil is replaced, the anti-freeze is checked. Why can't we take care of our souls the way we do our cars?"

After worship, one of his congregants wrung the rabbi's hand enthusiastically. "Rabbi, that was a great sermon. I'm really grateful to you. I had forgotten all about taking my car for a checkup." The rabbi had not learned the first lesson which every television producer knows: You never make the commercial better than the program.

* * *

On the eve of the Day of Atonement, when every observant Jew implores divine forgiveness for past sins, our family follows a traditional custom, just before the holy day candles are lit, of asking one another forgiveness for the hurts we inflicted during the past year. For Jewish law declares that only the transgressions committed against God are remitted by prayer. Transgressions against our fellow-men can only be atoned by an individual through a personally directed expression of remorse.

My wife and I were alone at dinner, preparing to begin the day-long Fast of Atonement when the phone rang. I grumbled my annoyance at the interruption. No one ever calls at that hour.

"Is this Morris Kertzer? I have an important matter I'd like to discuss with you. May I come to your home now?"

The caller evidently did not realize that he was shattering the sanctity of a solemn day. He introduced himself.

"My name is Mr. A., a manager of the New York Telephone Company. I understand that you've had trouble getting your name listed in our Information File since you moved to the city. Let me explain the trouble. Our computer made a mistake."

I interrupted the telephone executive to inform him that we were rushing to get ready for religious services. Besides, that computer explanation was nothing new.

"Mr. A., this is our Day of Atonement. I don't have time to talk just now. Can you call me back?"

"Mr. Kertzer, our computer misspelled your name, Ckertzer. The operators had to look it up under "C"".

I asked him if he knew of any language on earth which had words beginning with 'ck', and he fell back on the guilt of the wayward computer. But he was persistent.

The purpose of my call is this. I'd like to come over to express the regrets of the New York Telephone Company."

"But, Mr. A., your apology is enough. I accept it. This is our holiest day of the year. We're on our way to Temple and we'll be late."

"How about tomorrow morning? I'd like to do it personally."

"The Day of Atonement goes on all day tomorrow, Mr. A. Just send me a letter of apology. That's enough."

In a few moments, I stood in the pulpit of the Temple, donned in white robes, symbolic of our aspiration to purify our souls. And my text on personal forgiveness was at hand.

"Even the New York Telephone Company understands that the only way to seek forgiveness is by seeking out those we have wronged, meeting them face to face, and to plead, "I'm sorry!"

My Name Is Tora

"Dear friend," she wrote from her North Dakota home, "When I first found out that my name, Tora, had a holy meaning for the Jews, I was so tempted to go and see a Jewish rabbi and ask him to tell me about the Jews' Torah, but I just couldn't pick up the courage to do this.

"I started to pray to God to help me find out in some way. The next morning, my copy of Reader's Digest arrived in the mail and I thought what a wonderful way for God to answer my prayer. I have to tell you that this was the first time He answered. All the previous times I prayed, He didn't. (signed) Your friend, Tora."

Hundreds of letters came to my desk, in the summer of 1952, after my article, *What Is a Jew?*, appeared in *LOOK* magazine and *Reader's Digest.* Those responses came from every State in the Union and nearly every province of Canada. When the article was later published in a dozen foreign-language editions of the Digest, readers from all over the globe communicated their feelings about Jews and Judaism.

A letter from Brownsburg, Indiana, enclosed a self-addressed, stamped envelope. The writer, a woman, was intrigued by my explanation of the Jewish dietary laws relative to kosher meat. I had written that, for observant Jews, beef was ritually fit only if the animal was slaughtered without inflicting pain.

"Dear rabbi," she pleaded, "We have read what you had to say about kosher meat. We are not of your faith, but you can help us with our problem. We have had a cow in our family for a number of years. Unfortunately, the time has come to put her away. Will you send us, in the enclosed envelope, the name and address of a kosher slaughterer in Indianapolis, who will despatch her with tenderness, mercy and care. Gratefully yours,"

A Japanese army captain wrote a ten page letter from his home, which he listed as Kitayokota, Mutsoka-mura, Sanbu-gun, Chiba-Ken, Japan, to offer a few critical comments that reflected considerable thought. He wondered about the cogency of an ancient rabbinic saying which I had quoted, "Who is beloved by God, he who is beloved by Man." Did that always work? Hitler was beloved by millions of his countrymen. How did God feel? The prophets of the Bible were scorned by their people. How did God feel about them? Not easy questions to answer.

One foreign letter sent me to my world atlas to learn some facts about the country of its sender. The writer, Abdul Hahim Farhan, after reading the Arabic edition of Reader's Digest, presented a plan to solve the newly-created problem of Palestinian-Arab refugees. "We have a vast undeveloped country, the Sudan (which, I learned, to my amazement, from my map, covers almost one million square miles.) Soon, the British will be moving out, and we wish to retain the Moslem character of our nation. Today, we are outnumbered by the blacks in the South. If those Arab refugees were to be settled in the Sudan, we could solve both their problems and ours."

I forwarded his letter to officials in the United Nations. Later, I heard that the Arab League, as it was then called, showed no interest in Farhan's proposal. Since the days of my correspondence with Khartoum, I have followed news of the Sudan. My horror was compounded when I learned that the Sudanese Arabs later liquidated close to a half-million of the blacks in the South. Even more incredibly, I heard black American extremists repeat the absurdities of "third world" orators, who lauded the bonds that linked the black and Moslem peoples.

Many of my correspondents were Jews from small communities, in states like Kansas and Wyoming, who had only meagre access to information about Judaism; or from Christians who were curious about some aspect of the Jewish faith. One of the latter wrote, "Reading the Reader's Digest article, I discovered that I have been practising Judaism all my life without realizing it."

The responses often came by telephone. On two occasions, there was an almost mystical quality in their requests. A Lutheran minister, in the Far West, reacted to the article by initiating an investigation into his name. His surname had a Jewish ring to it, and he had done some probing into his family tree. After reading the article, and through further research, the pastor uncovered a family history that revealed a startling fact. In Budapest, in 1776, one of his paternal forefathers had left the Jewish faith to embrace Lutheranism. For some time, the Christian clergyman had considered the possibility of reverting to his ancestral religion. The magazine article had reinforced his impulse. How, he asked, could he take steps to undergo conversion?

A famous biologist came to my study, after he came upon my article in a dentist's office. (I discovered, from similar experiences, that dentists keep their magazines for at least two years.) He wanted more information about the Jewish religion. What was his motive? He wasn't sure. We spoke about his ancestry as I was curious about his surname. It ended with the vowel "o" which suggested a Latin background. The scientist was a third generation American, but two of his great-grandparents were born on the island of Malta.

Malta? That was interesting. I showed my guest a book about the Marranos, the "secret Jews" of Spain and Portugal, who had escaped the 15th century Inquisition by being baptized, but who continued to observe certain Jewish rites in the privacy of their homes. Some of these rituals were performed perfunctorily, their significance lost to the descendants of the Marranos. In 1492, the year of the expulsion of the Jews from Spain, some of the "secret Jews" had fled to Malta. Could the man, sitting before me, be of Marrano stock?

The biologist recalled a number of inexplicable customs which his grandfather practised. When the old man read aloud from some ancient books in his library, they had a Spanish sound. I told my visitor that there is a language, called Ladino, a medieval Spanish dialect, which is the counterpart of European Yiddish. Hundreds of thousands of Jews, whose roots are in Turkey, Greece, North Africa, and, more recently, Israel, write and speak Ladino.

My guest did not explain what had moved him to seek me out after the Digest article came to his attention. He didn't know himself. And, after my account of the Marranos who had come to Malta, he was more puzzled than ever. Could 1492 have reached out to pluck his ear in 1952?

* * *

The format of the article *What Is a Jew?*, and later, the expanded book by the same title, seemed to convey to readers that the author was a kind of answer man, a clerical "Dear Abby", because the presentation was in the form of questions and answers.

Following a television interview on CBS, the station loud speaker paged me, and I picked up a corridor phone. An angry caller shouted in my ear: "What are you doing about *capons?*"

"What should I be doing about capons?" I was stalling for time. It took me a few moments to focus on the thought that his concern was about poultry. He informed me in graphic earthy words that capons are castrated. My challenger had read in my book that Judaism is opposed to cruelty to animals. How did I propose to stop the poultry people from inflicting pain on helpless young chickens?

A phone call from a reader often involved an appeal to settle a domestic problem. Could I advise a mother about arranging the conversion of her future daughter-in-law to Judaism?

The couple came to my study. She was a Roman Catholic, and he was the product of an ultra-Orthodox home. He quoted Talmudic passages with ease. His mother had boasted about his training at the Flatbush Yeshivah, an all-day school, which had given him a splendid background in classical Jewish texts.

There was a complication. Both were college students, in graduate school, in an upstate New York community, and she was in her sixth month of pregnancy. They had visited an Orthodox rabbi in their community, but he had shown no interest in their situation. The young man knew all the Jewish legal aspects of their problem, and he quoted freely from Hebrew and Aramaic sources.

It occurred to me that the Reform rabbi in their city might be more flexible in training the girl for conversion, and marrying them, before the baby's arrival.

"What about Rabbi Goldblum in your town? I happen to know him, and he's a very understanding person."

"Goldblum? A Reform rabbi? This low I won't sink!"

* * *

Since the earliest days of television, I have appeared rather frequently on local and national broadcasts. During the late 1940's, I conducted a weekly religious program over a New York station, Channel 5. On a subway train, a woman, sitting opposite me, would cry out,

"Look, Gladys, I saw him on TV yesterday." She would hold up five fingers. "Channel 5? Right?" 7 6 — 2 5 4

My family appeared on several programs, during Jewish festivals and holyday seasons, including the *Tonight Show*, in its embryonic days, when the camera crew travelled from place to place to cover special interest stories. In one interview program, I asked the moderator, Arlene Francis, how many listeners were tuned in to the program. She, apologetically, ventured the estimate of six million. "It's a daytime show." Those astronomical figures fall lightly from the lips.

The day following the Arlene Francis show, I happened to attend a program at the Hollywood Bowl in California. I was engulfed in what seemed to be a never-ending sea of human beings, and the Bowl held only 20,000 people! Only yesterday morning, I had spoken to *three hundred* Hollywood Bowls! A modest television audience! At that time, Bishop Fulton Sheen was conducting a weekly telecast. His scintillating personality and brilliant insights were reaching into many more millions of homes. I once calculated that if, conceivably, St. Francis of Assisi, the preacher of the early thirteenth century, addressed a congregation of five hundred—a fair-sized congregation—every Sunday, for over seven hundred and fifty years, he would not be able to reach the numbers which the magnetic Bishop attracted in a *single* program!

There is nothing original in the thought that modern religious institutions have not yet adjusted to the realities of our mass media age. Professor McLuhan's message about the media has not been taken seriously by the Church and the Synagogue. The mainstream Church has made some feeble efforts in utilizing the media. The American Synagogue has not even begun to accommodate itself to the new world of communication. Paradoxically, the creative talent of many Jews has been poured into the mass media in extraordinary measure, but, with the exception of a single venture, *The Eternal Light,* none of it has been channeled into bringing the message of the Jewish faith to a mass audience.

In defense of their inertia, religious leaders cite the astronomical costs of telecasting. These are enormous. Labor Union rules help to skyrocket the costs. When I was asked by a small Wisconsin TV station to obtain a video-tape of a previous year's NBC Passover program, I was stymied by the regulation about 'residuals': the staff, involved in the old program, had to be reimbursed. Even more frustrating is the complex of unions involved in each minor aspect of production. In my weekly program, I usually had two chairs on the set. On one occasion, when I had two guests, instead of the usual one, I started to place my hands on a nearby chair. The producer cautioned,

"Drop that, rabbi. You have no union card."

"Joe," I said to an assistant producer nearby, "please push over that chair."

I might just as well have dropped a bomb. From behind the glass partition in the engineer's booth, the engineer's voice reminded me that Joe's union credentials did not include the right to move furniture. A member of that union was not scheduled to appear until *after* my program . . . After a few such frustrations, I developed the skill of slipping the toes of my shoes around the leg of a chair, while talking to my guests during rehearsal, and dragging it onstage. (I once gave a talk entitled, "Things They Never Taught Us at the Seminary.")

Spiritual values, I admit, are not commodities that can be marketed, as the saying goes, like soap. But, in moments of despair for the future outlook for religion in America, I have to confess that, when Walter Cronkite offers an ethical insight in two minutes of an ordinary weekday evening news broadcast, his audience embraces more *Jewish* listeners than all the worshippers in all the synagogues of America, even on the holiest day of the year. (I selected Walter Cronkite deliberately, because he holds a special place in the hearts of our family clan. He is an exact image of my father, David, of blessed memory. Hair-coloring, hair-line, facial features and all. When the CBS news comes on the air, my cousins, in different parts of the country and in Canada, call out: "Here comes Uncle Dave!")

My enthusiasm for the mass media was once dampened by an embarrassing experience. After that, I made a vow (never kept) not to permit a tape-recording of any speech of mine for radio use.

In 1951, I was invited by the producers of the NBC program, *Tex and Jinx*, to present a so-called sermonette. This program originated from Tex's and Jinx's Long Island home every weekday morning at eight o'clock, and lasted for one hour. My message was to be limited to one minute and a half. I managed to complete the tape in eighty-nine seconds.

What words of wisdom could I compress into eighty-nine seconds? I fell back on the inspiration of a text taken from the second century Talmudic "Ethics of the Fathers", a string of moral aphorisms.

The text was, "Judge not a man until thou standest in his place," the theme of tolerance in judgment. That took just a few seconds. Two or three more paragraphs of commentary filled in the rest of the time. The producer's office informed me that I would be notified when my sermonette was scheduled to be on the air.

Two weeks later, I tuned in to *660* on our kitchen radio. The opening format called for Tex and Jinx to scan the headlines in the *New York Times*. Jinx called attention to a picture that dominated the front page: the menacing figure of Senator Estes Kefauver, at that time, in the midst of a Senate investigation of crime. The Senator was pointing an accusing finger at New York's Mayor William O'Dwyer. "How do you explain, Mr. Mayor, what happened to the money which mysteriously disappeared and made its way into your office?"

Her husband assured Jinx that he knew his Honor, the Mayor, and had known him intimately for years. Tex spoke glowingly of Bill O'Dwyer as a man of impeccable integrity. The Senate investigator was on one of his "fishing expeditions". He had no right to challenge the mayor's honesty.

At that juncture, Jinx expressed her delight at the presence of their guest, Rabbi Morris Kertzer, who would offer a spiritual thought for today. I listened to myself declaring with fervor that "we ought to give every man the benefit of the doubt. Let's not be hasty in judging our neighbor. How wise were those old sages when they taught the lesson, "Judge not a man until thou standest in his place!" "

My two hosts applauded my bright, and altogether relevant, comments on the events of the day.

Jezebel in Hebrew School

Can you imagine a 20th century synagogue, of substantial size, whose regular worshippers numbered in the many hundreds, which had no religious school, nor any other facilities for the religious nurture of the congregants' children? My Bar Mitzvah was celebrated at the McCaul Synagogue in Toronto, to which my parents belonged, during the Feast of Tabernacles. Despite the fact that it was a weekday, the congregation consisted of well over a thousand worshippers. Yet, I had not received a single lesson in the Synagogue. In the 1920's, most children of traditional Jewish families attended a community school, called a Talmud Torah.

If a Jewish boy in my public school class told his classmates that he was enrolled in a *Religious* School, he would be regarded with suspicion: "Religion" was either a gentile word, or, worse still, a label attached to German Jews who had strayed into the shadowy world of Reform Judaism. Ordinary God-fearing children of God-fearing Jewish parents went to a Talmud Torah. Boys, from the age of six on, were students there every day but Friday, for at least ten hours a week of intensive study of the Hebrew language and Bible.

I was a student in the Euclid Avenue Hebrew School, a one-man enterprise conducted by Mr. Lubetsky, our "rebbe". (An appellation used without any suggestion of the sanctity associated with Hasidic leaders—a "rebbe" was simply a teacher.)

My memories of Mr. Lubetsky's personal appearance are vague. He seemed old and frail to me; however, he was no older than my parents. To cope with thirty or forty boys, for several after-school hours, when they had been released from the prison-house of the Canadian Public School of those days, was enough to generate battle fatigue and total nervous exhaustion.

Mr. Lubetsky wasn't old; he was tired. His bent posture was developed, not from poring over ancient texts, but from our torments. We emerged from the iron discipline of our public school. ("Bloom, stand in the corner, and face the wall for fifteen minutes; Schwartz, write on the blackboard twenty times: 'Neat boys use handkerchiefs.' Katz, don't slouch in your seat.") At the day's end, when all the liberated Italian and Irish boys were playing in the snow, we Jewish boys had stored up sufficient energy to martyrize the gentle Mr. Lubetsky.

Our Bible lessons, from the Book of Deuteronomy, warned us that there was a punishment for every crime. But, we operated with impunity. The Lubetsky family lived on the second floor, which we explored only rarely; and they stored their food, especially their preserves, in the basement—our playground. An old Hebraic tradition—well over two thousand years old—counsels the first-grade teacher to feed his pupils honey-cakes, shaped in the letters of the Hebrew alphabet, so that the children's association with learning will be one of sweetness. My earliest association with learning is related to the aroma of dill pickles. During our basment forays, we would plunge our arms deep into the brine of the rebbe's pickle-barrel. How we managed to escape detection, when we trooped back into the classroom after recess, I will never understand. The pickles were gone, but the dill must have lingered on. Mr. Lubetsky was probably too weary to fight back!

When the snows came, the rebbe's wife would return with peace of mind to her washing and cooking. For the *Cheder* boys (we used the Old World word for Hebrew School) moved out of doors for street-hockey, or, more often, snowball war. Our rebbe might preach to us to be like Aaron of the Bible, "loving peace and pursuing peace," and we would memorize his lesson to perfection; and then, we would launch our war-games.

We refined the art of snow-ball manufacture: Cup the snow in your bare hands; let it melt slowly into a fine ball; permit it to harden into a missile that has both the texture and the color of solid ice. Casualties were heavy on both sides. Our mothers found it difficult to understand how a boy could acquire a black eye in a Bible class.

Our Hebrew School was not one hundred per cent masculine. The rebbe's daughter, Lummy, (a diminutive of Shulamith), was the only girl in my class. At the age of eleven, Lummy was tall, blonde, and wore her hair in an intriguing (at least to me) Buster-Brown style. She sat next to me on our bench, (we had no individual seats) towering over the rest of us eleven-year-olds. Lummy had my heart, in the palm of her hand, every day from four to six-thirty.

As the teacher's daughter, and the only girl in the class, Lummy had a unique perogative. She had the exclusive use of a Bible that contained an English translation. The rest of us held large, unwieldy Hebrew Bible texts and commentaries. The typical lesson involved translation, not into English, but Yiddish, which we all understood fairly well, but, not infrequently, the translation was as mystifying as the original Hebrew. Armed with her English translation, Lummy sometimes introduced me into the glamorous world of forbidden words, words glossed over by her father with studied casualness.

One day, we were reading the second chapter of the Book of Joshua. It was the story of the Battle of Jericho, in which Joshua's spies gained entrance into the fortress city. Once inside, they visited the house of *ishah zonah*. Mr. Lubetsky gingerly translated the biblical text: the spies came "to the home of a grocery woman". That seemed quite natural to an eleven year old. The first place to visit when you come into a town is the grocery store.

Lummy nudged her elbow into my ribs, and surreptitiously slid her book into my field of vision. Her eyes darted from me to the words at the tip of her fingers: "the house of a *harlot.*" What was a "harlot"? Neither Lummy nor I knew. But her glance intimated that the young Jezebel had inveigled me into the exciting realm of taboo. We revelled in our secret. Lummy and I were the only two in the whole class who knew that Joshua's spies never saw the inside of a Jericho grocery-store.

One day, Mr. Lubetsky announced that we were going to have an extra-curricular activity—a Young Judea Club of our own. We were now the Junior part of the Zionist Organization of Canada. The Buds of Judah Club, modelled after the Benevolent Associations of our parents, had all the trimmings of their adult organizations: officers, dues, minutes of meetings, a constitution, and regular weekly meetings. Our dues were to be one cent a week.

I was elected president for ten consecutive terms of office. The signal honor was related to my financial status. I had earned a quarter delivering handbills for our corner grocery-store, and, on an impulse which I regretted for a year, I paid my dues for twenty-four weeks in advance. Naturally, too, I was captain of one of our debating teams.

Mr. Lubetsky organized a debate on the theme: "Shall Jews Return to Zion?" As president, I chose the popular side, the affirmative. Each of the four speakers—two on each side—was allowed three to five minutes of argument. The judges, two post-Bar Mitzvah boys, ruled that my side had lost, thirty-five arguments to thirty-three. The only detail that clings to my memory was the one that caused our downfall.

"Why should we return to Palestine?" I shouted. "Because, as our rebbe told us, there are mountains in Zion. Maybe there's gold in those hills."

My opponent wasted no time in a counter-attack: "Maybe there ain't." Incontrovertible.

* * *

Bar Mitzvah training for our thirteenth birthday was a routine matter for students of the Euclid Avenue Hebrew School. Even my speech was delivered in Hebrew. Our knowledge of the language was sufficient for us to master the intricacies of the Bible portion, the blessings, the chants, all within a five or six week period. Except for the brief speech, all other parts of the ceremony were chanted, and we were very familiar with the melodies.

All, except for one student, Henry Siegal. Henry was a monotone. To be a Bar Mitzvah monotone is far worse a disaster than being a color-blind artist. Our suffering was no less than his. Instead of having to listen to Henry for six weeks, we were subjected to his rehearsal for six months. Fate mocked us, too, in the selection of Henry's Prophetic Passage, assigned by tradition for that particular Sabbath in November. It was the first chapter of the First Book of Kings; the story of David in his declining years. The opening words of the Book depict the royal servants worrying about their master's poor blood circulation. "Now, King David was old, and stricken in years, and, though they covered him, he could not keep warm."

David's servants prescribed, "Let a young virgin stand

before the king, and lie in thy bosom, that our lord, the King, may keep warm."

Within two months, the entire class, with the exception of Henry, knew the first chapter of Kings I, including the melody, by heart. We found ourselves, absent-mindedly, humming the melody, and, later, chanting the words everywhere we went; on the playground at school, in the street, and at home. My parents, aunts and uncles, who understood Hebrew, were shocked by my biblical vocalizing. The McPherson boy next door, and Nora Mulligan, across the road, were content to sing, "When Francis Dances With Me." But their child had to run through the neighborhood chanting: "Let a young virgin lie in thy bosom, that our lord, the King, may keep warm."

More than half a century has passed. Once in a while, as I walk alone, I find myself humming and chanting the song of Henry Siegal.

Healer from Iowa

I heard about Doctor Arthur Steindler almost the first day I came to teach at the University of Iowa. I first saw him in a ward of the Children's Hospital, when I brought in a group of college students to entertain the young patients. Down the corridor, at a fast clip, walked a man in white, followed breathlessly by some twenty-five residents and internes. He was then in his early sixties, close to six feet in height, with gray-black hair and mustache, brown eyes, and rather bushy eyebrows.

There was something unusual about the twenty-five youthful doctors who hovered around their teacher. Two were Japanese-Americans, and, after Pearl Harbor, Dr. Steindler needed all his persuasive talents to allow them to continue their studies while all other members of their race had been interned for security reasons. One member of the group was a Siamese, several others were Spaniards, Latin-Americans and Filipinos. All had come to study under Steindler, who was regarded as the Einstein of orthopedic surgery.

So far as I know, he had the unique distinction of being an "alma mater" in himself. On the roster of the Arthur Steindler Alumni Association, over three hundred surgeons are listed. In his lifetime, one out of six American surgeons who devoted their lives to the

maimed and the crippled, acquired their skills from the
Iowa doctor. And, today, in a score of foreign countries,
the techniques used in combatting osteomyelitis (bone
tumor), polio, club feet, scoliosis (curvature of the spine),
and scores of other afflictions were perfected under
Steindler's guidance.

One day, I saw Arthur Steindler pacing up and down
the corridor of the Children's Hospital. His eyes were
half-closed, and his face drawn as if in great pain. I asked
one of the staff members what was wrong.

"Nothing particular," was the reply. "After a heavy
operating schedule, he looks that way. He suffers pain
along with his patients—especially the children."

For a man who had performed over 30,000 operations,
that was a lot of anguish. The doctor once showed me a
reprint of a paper he delivered to a Medical Society. It
was entitled, "The Symphony of Pain." His colleagues,
he reminded them, ought to remember that they were
not treating muscles, bones, tendons and ligaments, but
human beings, sensitive to suffering.

On occasion, I enjoyed walking "rounds" with him.
The youngsters in the wards, in traction and embedded
in casts—some of whom I would see from one end of the
year to the other—would brighten up as they watched
his approach. His was no contrived bedside manner:
they stretched out their toes or their fingers so that the
doctor would touch them.

Arthur Steindler, the son of a distinguished jurist, was
born in Austria. His early ambition was to emulate his
father in a law career. But, the judge handed down a
decision in his home: "Arthur, you will study medicine
in Prague." And he did. In 1907, he came to America,
despite the world-wide reputation which Vienna held as
medical research center, especially in his chosen field of
orthopedics.

Years later, a Cedar Rapids couple brought their child to the Vienna Clinic for treatment of a serious deformity. They were told that they need not have travelled all the way to Austria. There was a man, only twenty-five miles away from Cedar Rapids, who knew as much as any one in the world about that disease.

My fascination for my neighbor led me to probe into his background. I knew that he was responsible for the magnificent Children's Hospital, made possible by Rockefeller funds. So far as I knew, there was nothing like it in the United States. In 1913, a very forward-looking Iowa legislature had passed the Perkins Law, establishing a medical center in the tiny community of Iowa City. Every morning, as we looked out our window, we would see a stream of ambulances bringing patients from every part of the State—some of them from Sioux City, 350 miles away. Many ambulances brought orthopedic patients; it did not take too many years before every farmer in Iowa knew the name of Arthur Steindler, the miracle worker.

A *Des Moines Register* feature story told of a thirty-one year-old polio victim, who had not taken a step since she was ten. After Steindler's treatment, she walked out of the hospital, unaided. Another story told of Beulah, a pretty sixteen year-old girl, who had been hurt when she crashed into a wall in a basketball game. She went into a coma for six weeks. The diagnosis was encephalitis, sleeping sickness, and her physician recommended that she be kept permanently in a wheel chair, since she would look grotesque, even if she were able to master a little locomotion. Dr. Steindler infused new hope in her family. After an ordeal of forty operations, Beulah learned to walk with a cane. She was happily married, the mother of three children.

In view of the fact that many of his cases required

lengthy treatment, the State grew impatient at the financial burden. Then, the doctor would take some of his patients into his home.

The Steindler household was more like a hostel. The doctor and his wife had no loving children of their own, but, in the wake of Nazi persecution, a steady stream of refugees, nieces, nephews, cousins, poured into Iowa City. The Steindlers added a wing to their gracious home to accomodate the newcomers. At one time, there were thirty guests.

The doctor met a girl in the hallway of his home. "Who are you?" he asked.

"I'm one of the relatives you brought over from Europe, living here."

"Welcome. Make yourself at home."

Our own home was often the gathering place for some of the residents. They worshipped their mentor, and repeated stories of his miracles. Dr. Steindler had shown them, for example, how to get one muscle to do the work of another, when it became useless. The textbooks called it "the Steindler physiological tendon transplant"—and described how an injured thumb, that could not be bent, could be made as good as new.

It was Steindler who introduced to America new methods of treating club feet, the congenital crippler of boys, described in Somerset Maugham's *Of Human Bondage*. So, too, he brought new hope to victims of curvature of the spine. In my childhood, I saw so many of both. Was it possible that my neighbor had changed the course of childhood medical history?

The doctor, who brought healing to thousands, had his own share of personal grief. A young member of his family was killed when his auto crashed into the side of a train. Arthur Steindler returned from the cemetery, and went directly to his beloved piano. Like so many men of genius, his talents in his avocation, music, were far above average. He sat for hours, seeking comfort in Brahms, Schumann and Rachmaninoff. In his youthful days, he had accompanied his friend, Albert Einstein, as the physicist played the violin.

At the outbreak of World War I, the Austrian-born surgeon tried to enlist, but he was ineligible; Austria was enemy territory. The Army finally relented, and immediately sought his counsel. Lt. Colonel Steindler was asked: What is the maximum weight a soldier can carry on his back without injury? What is the best pace for a soldier? Dr. Steindler was dispatched to factories in Massachusetts to help design the most comfortable shoes for the Army, and the best texture for sox. It was not quite on a par with designing tanks and submarines, but it was the immigrant's way of repaying his adopted country for its hospitality.

Iowa folklore is filled with Steindler saga. A number of years ago, in a strange way, I caught a glimpse of his reputation as a wonder worker. I shared a lecture platform in Omaha, Nebraska, with an eminent Bible scholar, Professor *Steiner* of Grinnell College in Iowa. When we returned to our hotel room, the hall was filled with mothers and crippled children. They had heard that Professor *Steindler* of Iowa was in Omaha. The Old Testament authority explained to the disappointed mothers that he was somewhat of an expert on Bible miracles, but that he was not the Doctor Steindler with the miraculous hands.

The Case of Murder by Chicken Soup

Judge Gaffney had been on the bench for over thirty years. He thought that he had witnessed every aspect of human nature, from the depths of depravity to the heights of nobility. But the case before him was a puzzler. It made no sense. The defendant was a "rabbi"! Not, technically, a rabbi: they called him Rev. Rubin. The Jews of his small Iowa town could not afford the services of a full-time spiritual leader, and the Rev. Rubin took care of many of their ritual needs: he provided religious training for a handful of children; served as Cantor; handled ritual circumcisions; and, on occasion, even kosher slaughtering.

Rev. Rubin and his wife lived in an apartment above a store operated by one of their married sons. They were quiet people, soft-spoken, and on friendly terms with their neighbors. With one exception: Mrs. Kathleen Gilligan. No one knew the cause of the friction between the Jewish functionary and his Irish neighbor, but every one was aware that the two families had ceased to greet each other in the street.

One Friday morning in July, as Mrs. Gilligan was passing the Rubin store, she felt a sharp burning pain on the elbow of her right arm, the searing heat of boiling water that seemed to rain down from the sky. She instinctively leaped into the roadway, missing the full force of the cascading liquid. Her screams drew a small crowd of passersby and store customers who gathered around her. Luckily, the torrent that came from above had dropped harmlessly to the sidewalk. It was not boiling water, but soup; in fact, boiling chicken soup.

The crowd looked up to the second floor, and noticed that the window of the Rubin apartment was wide-open. Mrs. Gilligan knew at once who had tried to kill her by scalding: the Jewish "rabbi".

When the case came to trial before Judge Gaffney, the plaintiff painted a vivid picture of the tension between the two families: quarrels between the children; the damage done to the Gilligan rose-bushes by the Rubin dog; and the words of recrimination between the two women. She had never spoken to the Rev. Rubin. Indeed, she was under the impression that he was a fairly decent sort of person. Then, came the unprovoked attack by boiling chicken soup.

The Rev. Rubin, a rather timid man, under the deft guidance of his defense attorney, described the events leading up to the unfortunate accident. That hot July morning, Mrs. Rubin was cooking the evening Sabbath meal. At the same time, she was also preparing her husband's breakfast. The Rev. Rubin liked hot milk to pour over his cereal. He happened to walk into the kitchen, and discovered that his wife had inadvertently let the pan of milk boil over—into the chicken soup. For an observant Jew, milk and meat must never be mixed. The Bible specifically forbids it. He rushed toward the stove, impulsively picked up the pot of soup, ignoring the risk of burning himself, and hurled the tainted soup out the open window!

Mrs. Gilligan and her attorney, Jim O'Brien, listened to the Rubin story incredulously. As a matter of fact,

Judge Gaffney found it hard to follow the defendant's reasoning, and invited him to explain his action in greater detail. The Rev. Rubin cited three verses from the Bible, two from Exodus, and one from Deuteronomy.

At that point, the courtroom was transformed into a kind of Bible session. The Mosaic law states: "Thou shalt not seethe a kid in its mother's milk." Out of that single mystifying verse, came the impulse to rain boiling chicken soup on to an Iowa street?

I sat in Judge Gaffney's chambers, years after the trial, as he unfolded the climax of the story. After intensive investigation, he found the defendant's defense credible, and declared the Rev. Rubin, not guilty.

The intervening years had dimmed his recollection of the arguments presented by the defendant. Granted that Jews, who observe the dietary laws, would not eat food containing both milk and meat at the same time. But, what would arouse the emotions of a Jew, merely contemplating the sight of boiling milk and boiling chicken soup on the same stove? Judge Gaffney could not figure that out.

My own explanation seemed feeble, as I attempted to convey to my friend the emotions attached to traditional adherence to kosher laws. If he were a student of Talmudic law, dating back two thousand years, he would read in minute detail that the dietary laws extended far beyond the food itself. In the case he cited, the offending vessels could never be used again, and would have to be discarded.

The Judge stroked his forehead. To attach that much emotion to food laws seemed quite irrational. Only the reputation of Rev. Rubin as a gentle human being, had saved him. There could be no imputation of malice on his part. Assault by chicken soup was surely alien to his character. Still, what was all the excitement?

The case of Gilligan versus Rubin reminded me of the thousands of problems that have been presented to a unique tribunal in New York City, called the Jewish Conciliation Board. I told Judge Gaffney that the courts of New York, with its tremendous Jewish population, often referred this type of case to the Board. Of course, only when all the litigants were Jewish.

For the past fifty years, the Board has been adjudicating disputes between Jewish individuals or organizations. Recently, the writer, James Jaffe, wrote a book, *So Sue Me.*, reporting his experiences in covering a number of these "trials". In Jaffe's words, the court deals with matters of social Jewish concern that might be incomprehensible to non-Jewish judges."

In speaking with the Iowa judge, I cited a legal battle with far more ritual subtlety than his "attempted murder by chicken soup" case.

"As a judge, what would you do in a suit of an elderly Jew against a hospital in New York, asking for a huge sum of money for damages inflicted in the disposal of an amputated foot, following surgery. According to Jewish tradition, an amputated limb had to be buried in a cemetery plot. The plaintiff had elicited a promise from the hospital authorities, prior to surgery, that they would provide proper burial of the foot in a plot which he had purchased for himself and his wife. Apparently, a negligent employee had followed normal hospital procedures in disposing of the limb.

"The plaintiff now argues that, according to Jewish tradition—at least, mystical tradition—on the Day of Resurrection, he would return to life eternal, minus one foot. As a result of the hospital's negligence, he was condemned to hobble through eternity on one foot! Surely a settlement in the millions of dollars was not adequate compensation for the anguish, grief, humiliation and discomfort of such a prospect."

How was the case settled by the Board—which consisted of the regular panel of attorney, rabbi and businessman—in a way to satisfy the aggrieved party?

As I recall, the three men, selected for their wide experience and tactfulness, agreed that the plaintiff's charges should not be treated lightly. His beliefs were to be respected, and the hospital ought to be penalized in some *material* way. On the other hand, the injury inflicted upon the plaintiff was spiritual rather than material. Therefore, the amount of damages finally determined, several hundred dollars, was to be turned over to a Home for Aged Sages in Jerusalem. Thus, both he and the hospital would receive Divine consideration for their joint act of benevolence.

Judge Gaffney agreed that my "heavenly disability" case was even more complex and challenging than his "chicken soup" case.

The Emperor's Candlesticks

One of the tragic dimensions of the Nazi holocaust which I have never heard mentioned is that the Jews of Germany and Austria, whom Hitler liquidated, were probably the most German-loving segment of their Fatherland. Jews in every country are not only loyal citizens, but they manifest a passionate devotion for their homelands. Especially do they embrace its culture. The German-speaking Jews went beyond passion. Theirs was an intoxication with everything German: its literature, its music, its art, its life-style. When they spoke the language, they caressed the words. Although they retained their religious roots, the Jews of Hamburg and Frankfurt and Vienna carried on an intense love-affair with the landscape, the history, the traditions and the very accents of their beloved homelands.

In 1936, I travelled with over three hundred Viennese Jews on a visit to Palestine. On shipboard, we Americans engaged in interminable debates with our Austrian co-religionists over the prospects of *Anschluss*, Hitler's taking over his native country. Only two years later, history was to vindicate our fears, but our fellow-passengers could not conceive of such a possibility.

"Frau Katz," I suggested to our table-mate, as our ship neared the shores of the Holy Land, "you're visiting your children in Haifa. Why don't you ask them about cashing in your return ticket? You can't have any future in Vienna."

Frau Katz's determination to return to what was probably a trip to the gas chamber was not grounded in an "it can't happen here" psychology. She simply loved all things German: the texture of its life, the air she breathed in her native land. Despite the fact that a number of her friends had already moved to Palestine and were now publishing a small German-language weekly called, "In Exile."

The late Professor Kurt Lewin, one of the most eminent social psychologists of our time, a founder of the *Gestalt* school, recalled to me his experiences in the early days of Hitler when he was still able to teach at the University of Berlin.

One of Professor Lewin's Jewish colleagues, who was head of the Department of German Languages and Civilization at the University, had won a national reputation as an authority on Germanic culture. He knew virtually every inch of his beloved *Vaterland,* from Prussia to Bavaria, and he infected his students of over more than a generation with his enthusiasm for the world that counted: the world of Goethe, Schiller and Heine. When he entered his Berlin classroom, one morning, a Brown-shirted student caustically called the professor's attention to some words which his Nazi students had scribbled on the blackboard.

"Raus schweine Jude!" (Get out, swine of a Jew!)

The brilliant scholar did not utter a word. With quiet deliberation, he stuffed his notes into his brief-case, strode out of the lecture hall, and, with the erect posture of his Prussian officer training, made his way to his office. There, he blew out his brains!

* * *

Like many Jews, in the years following World War II, I have avoided Germany and Austria in my European travels. In the early post-war years, Jewish tourists, who visited Cologne and Frankfurt or Salzburg, would see in the faces of passers-by the image of storm troopers. With the birth of a new generation, both German-Austrian and Jewish, a considerable amount of this sensitivity has evaporated.

When I arrived on a visit to Vienna, I registered at the Hotel Imperial, without too much misgiving over the fact that it had served as Gestapo Headquarters. (A few years earlier, as an officer stationed in France, I was billeted at a hotel which had been used by the Gestapo during the war. Their stationery was still in my night table. Our midnight-to-morning hotel clerk wore a Hitler-type mustache, and was built just like the Fuerer. We occasionally wondered if the Nazi dictator might still be alive, wearing the most perfect disguise, none at all.)

In Vienna, a visit to the resplendent Schonbrunn Palace, located at the edge of the Austrian capital, kindled many childhood memories for me. I walked through a half-mile of beautifully appointed salons which displayed the priceless collection of the Emperor Francis Joseph and his family. These included the *objets d'art* accumulated by his ambitious ancestor, the Empress Marie-Theresa.

In my childhood, the name of Kaiser Franz-Josef, as my parents called him, was as familiar to me as that of our next-door neighbor. As children of recent immigrants, we heard stories of the old world royalty as a part of kitchen conversation. Metaphors were bandied about which were filled with allusions to the royal family that ruled over the great Austro-Hungarian Empire. Virtually, they were honorary members of the family. Kaiser

Franz Josef was part of the background of my parents' entire lives.

This monarch ruled for over sixty-eight years, even longer than Queen Victoria. He was nicknamed by Austrian anti-semites, 'einer Judenfreund'', a friend of the Jews. Unlike the despised Czars of Russia, this sovereign insisted on granting rights to his Jewish subjects. When an antisemitic mayor was elected in Vienna, Franz Josef conferred a high honor on the Chief Rabbi in order to show his support for the Jews. On the annual Sabbath devoted to blessing the Emperor, Austrian synagogues were filled to over-flowing. At times, he attended Jewish worship.

My mother explained the reason for his longevity. The prophet Elijah appeared to Franz Josef and promised him long life, for his many acts of kindness to the Jewish people.

We children were told that the domain of the emperor was so vast that it extended deep into the heart of Russo-Poland right to the very door-steps of my mother's native village.

It was with more than a little awe that I held in my hands, a few years ago, two magnificent sterling silver candelabra which had once belonged to the Kaiser Franz-Josef of my childhood. A close friend had lent them to me for a day.

The story of those candlesticks reflects in microcosm the 20th century history of European Jewry.

My friend, who owned the candelabra, had roots in Vienna that were more than two centuries old. One of her forefathers, an 18th century Austrian rabbi, is regarded by Jewish historians as one of the primary authorities in Jewish religious law. His decisions, called responsa, are cited by contemporary authorities as binding upon observing Jews.

How did the Schonbrunn silver candlesticks come into the possession of a Viennese Jewish family? My friend's grandfather had been a dealer in antique silver. Early in the century, a flaw was discovered in the silver, and the candelabra were sold to her grandfather.

In 1937, a year before *Anschluss*, my friend's family, with prescience, saw the beginning of the end for Austrian Jewry. Through Christian friends, the treasured silver was smuggled into Switzerland, and held in Zurich for safekeeping. The first branch of the family to escape managed to reach England, but they arrived, stripped of all their possessions. In London, when the refugees received the candelabra, they promptly pawned them, in order to establish a catering business. After their venture had prospered, they redeemed the Schonbrunn treasure.

A second branch of the Viennese family, also without resources, found a home in Tel Aviv. Their London relatives shipped the silver to Israel, and the same routine followed: the pawnshop, success in their new business, redemption.

A third branch of the clan, who had wandered from haven to haven, finally settled in New York City. They duplicated the formula of their Israeli and English kinsmen. At long last, the candelabra were liberated permanently.

Here they were on my desk for a day. I scrutinized the delicate detail of their design, the creation of a master silversmith who must have loved his craft. Their unusual beauty and the drama of their world-wide peregrinations were very exciting, but my emotions were stirred for a more personal reason. I was touching the sterling-silver candlesticks that had once belonged to my parents' personal friends, Franz Josef and his beautiful empress, rulers over most of Continental Europe.

The outer reaches of that Empire, according to my mother, touched her childhood home. As an adventurous teen-ager, Mother would dive into the Bug River, and swim underwater, to escape detection by the Emperor's border guards, in order to land for a few moments and place her feet on the soil of the romantic empire.

And here I was, three-quarters of a century later, clasping Franz Josef's very own candlesticks between my fingers!

A Child's Eye View
of a Clergyman

I invited a kindergarten class to visit our sanctuary in a magnificent Temple in the heart of Manhattan. I explained all the major symbols: an elaborately fashioned Menorah—the traditional candelabrum—the ornate Eternal Light, the Ten Commandments, etched in gold on white marble, and the colorful stained-glass windows.

The following week, their teacher handed me a sheaf of drawings which the tiny tots had made in response to her suggestion that they re-create in crayon what they had seen in the sanctuary. Every single drawing had captured the outstanding feature in their memory: the microphone, to which I had not called their attention.

Jean Piaget was right. The Swiss psychologist tells us that the eyes of childhood have little in common with adult eyes. Children see the world through an entirely different perspective than their elders. I would go one step beyond Piaget. The emotional perceptions of young children are altogether unlike those of adults. I have observed, over a period of forty years in the rabbinate, the beauty, the unalloyed charm, and the heart-tugging openness of children from three to nine; and I have followed them to prosaic adulthood, with an interlude of adolescence, a period in which the transients prepare themselves for the banalities of adulthood by wearing all kinds of masquerade costumes, perhaps in imitation of their primitive ancestors. The current species of *homo sapiens* seems to have reversed the processes of nature: they are transformed from butterfly-children into cater-pillar-adults. I sometimes wonder if the original Garden of Eden design was different.

As the Bible might have said: "A little child can teach them." Many rabbis have abandoned the custom of wearing robes in the pulpit. Perhaps they have heard reactions similar to those of a four-year-old in my congregation:

"Mommy, why does the rabbi wear a lady's long nightgown?"

My feeling that children possess an instinct for essentials led me to explore the images which they have of a rabbi. I invited the children of my Religious School, from the fourth, fifth and sixth grades, to write down their thoughts on the subject: "What Is a Rabbi For?" Their comments, written in the classroom without prior notice, were spontaneous and unrehearsed.

Some time later, I sought the assistance of Protestant ministers and Roman Catholic priests to learn what images the youngsters in their churches entertain of their clergymen.

Of the three faith-groups, as might be expected, the Catholic children, who were exposed to the presence of their pastor more than the others, had a realistic perception of the clergyman's role. They expressed an affection for their priest, and, often, a desire to emulate him. One boy of nine wrote of his dream of becoming a priest, maybe even a pope or a bishop some day. A boy, one year his senior, articulated his enthusiasm for a priestly vocation: "I'd like my young brother to be a priest!" Obviously, he had studied the Bible, for he concluded his last sentence: "Thus enduth this paragraph."

Protestant children seem to have the least clear-cut perception of the role of the minister. Possibly, his title is the least descriptive. The words, rabbi, and priest have no other connotation. But there are cabinet ministers, and various people who *minister* to all kinds of needs. Some of the youngsters characterize their minister as a sort of priest. But their general visualization is of a man who works only on Sundays, who preaches and teaches about God and Jesus, and concerns himself with congregants in trouble—the poor; those with problems. They are people you talk to when your feelings are hurt, wrote one nine-year-old.

A Jewish child, of the same age, depicts the rabbi as a man who sits in a room with wall-to-wall carpeting and makes compliments. His Protestant peer sees him in the pulpit putting his hands up and down so we know when to sit down and when to stand up.

Do synagogue and church children think of their pastor as being of a different breed of human being? A Catholic youngster acknowledges: "No one should mess around when a priest is talking." A Jewish child envisions his rabbi as having a special pipe-line: "The rabbi talks to God and tells us what He is thinking." His classmate, a girl, waxes eloquent: "Garbed in ceremonial robes, he makes you feel that you are really in contact with God. (A Catholic theme, too.) To give pleasure to the things you do every day, he tells a witty tale, usually one that gives the simple task of daily life true meaning and usefulness."

To the child, the pastor represents the conscience of the congregation. "Priests teach us not to be mean and rotten." To a Protestant girl, her minister is one "who tells people not to kill people, and helps people to find themselves through the word of God." The priest may be a Robin Hood in Roman garb. "They give money to the poor which they get from the rich." Many children would agree with the Jewish boy, to whom "a rabbi is a standard for which people live around."

Few of the children seem to have gleaned the lesson of ecumenism. Although one Catholic youngster imagines that "God uses priests so his love will get around," his class-mate writes that, "Priests teach about God, Abraham, Moses and other Catholics."

On the whole, the children of all faiths see their pastors as ordinary human beings, even if, in the words of a Protestant nine-year-old, her minister is "like one of the twelve decipals and we are his sheep." Despite the clerical garb of the priest, there seems to be little emotional distance between the youngster and his pastor. "Priests are just ordinary men that were called by God to be his special servants. They are not appointed by some one. They are people who love God so much that they want to spread his work." A Jewish child shares the view: "People think he does nothing but religious things, but he does visit hospitals—imagine all the money he spends on flowers—whew!"

What do children think their pastors do all week? The Protestant youngster has a rather vague notion of the minister's functions in the church. One of them envisions him as thinking and thinking all week on what he will say on Sunday. A sixth-grade student in the Temple school dramatizes his ideas:

"The business man awakens every morning with a feeling of impending doom, he has to complete an account with a customer. A rabbi awakens on a Monday with a feeling of impending doom. He has only five days to complete his sermon for next Sabbath."

Several children commiserate with their pastor:

"A rabbi's work is never done. Who else do you call on in time of joy, weddings, bar mitzvahs, holy days and the

like, and, yes, even funerals? Your friendly, neighborhood rabbi. There are no hours you can't speak to him.
It must be very difficult to be a rabbi's wife. She must be
a giving and tolerant person. When people argue they
come to a rabbi to settle it. He probably is very scared
sometimes." A younger child believes that "a rabbi
would like to trade jobs for something easier. But I think
he loves his work."

Some of the students in my New York Religious
School were, apparently, thinking of becoming script
writers for television comedians:

"Most people think a rabbi's life is different than others. But it isn't. Like a sanitation worker, he helps people
to get rid of problems. A sanitation worker makes house
calls. So does a rabbi. Only a sanitation worker usually
gets off on Saturdays."

Another aspiring script-writer:

"A rabbi sleeps every night, but so do ministers, so
that is irrelevant. He comes to Temple at 12:30. On Tues-
days he works on a sermon. On Thursday he puts finish-
ing touches on his sermon. On Friday he eats dinner and
gives his sermon. He should have a bullet-proof shield
around the pulpit standing there within shooting-
range."

One of my young students was worried about the rabbi's diet: "A rabbi has special breakfasts, lunches and
dinners. AM I GLAD I DON'T have to do all that."

Protestant, Catholic and Jewish children all draw an
essentially human image of their spiritual leader. He is
their guide and mentor. In the words of a Protestant girl:
"he is friendly, honest, kind and considerate and teaches
about God and Jesus so that we can find happiness and
answers to problems." To the Catholic child, he may
"hear confession and a lot of stuff. But he has fun and
doesn't stick around in bed. He is invited to parties."

The most eloquent tribute to a rabbi came from the pen of a thirteen-year-old boy: "He gives the young boy the courage to face adulthood. He has a kind word for everybody. There is a specialness about him that makes it easier to speak to him. And he doesn't tell your parents that you've got a problem."

A youngster in a Religious School, with a flair for precision, wrote his views under the title of "A Rabbi's Schedule for the Day":

"3:30 a.m.   Who knows?
 9:30 a.m.   Prepare for speech.
10:00 a.m.   Give speech at a breakfast
11 a.m.   Parents Meeting
Noon   Rehearse for funeral
1 p.m.   Proceed with funeral
2 p.m.   Wedding
3:30 p.m.   Visit ill WIDOW
1 a.m.   Home to his wife."

(The widow must have been very ill.)

An occasional infelicitous use of the English language may restore a clergyman's humility.

"What is the job of a rabbi? He agonizes services for young and old. He also agonizes classes."

I have known few clergymen whose egos have not been deflated by the "slings and arrows" of some of their less thoughtful congregants. But, their spiriits are sustained by rewarding encounters with bright-eyed, guileless youngsters, in their midst, who are filled with a sense of awe and wonder about their universe; and, somehow, through a kind of childhood alchemy, associate that awe and wonder with those who don their Creator's uniform. These heaven-eyed youngsters see in their pastor, as one Protestant child expressed it: *"a teacher of all good things,* a friend, a real friend."

Sholom Aleichem and My Father

My Jerusalem cousin, Abigail, once mentioned in an off-hand way that her father was a cousin of Sholom Aleichem, the world's greatest Jewish humorist, the Mark Twain of Yiddish literature. I found it hard to believe.

"Do you mean that my father was related to him, too?"

"Naturally. As a matter of fact, I seem to remember that your grandfather and Sholom Aleichem played together as children."

When I returned home, I visited Toronto where my Aunt Esther lived. Dad was gone, but his sister would be able to confirm Abigail's statement.

"Aunt Esther, Cousin Abigail told me that your father was a cousin of Sholom Aleichem. Is it true?"

"What a question! He was your grandfather's cousin."

It seemed incredible. My father, David, was an insurance agent, but he wrote extensively for Yiddish newspapers and magazines. In fact, he had written several profiles of the Yiddish humorist, but I could not recall any reference to our kinship.

"Aunt Esther, why didn't you ever tell us?"

Her answer was classic Sholom Aleichem: "You never asked!"

This happened a few years before *Fiddler On the Roof*

became a part of contemporary culture. Audiences in Finland, Germany, Japan, and in virtually every country which had a theater, drew the character of Tevyeh to their hearts, without realizing that he was the product of the whimsical imagination of a Jewish writer who preferred the pen-name, Sholom Aleichem, to Rabinowitz, his family name.

It seemed almost unbelievable to me that my kinship with the humorist was derived through my father, because Dad was always serious about everything. Much more credible would have been a kinship through Mother. She was the one who saw the comic in life. Perhaps she had managed to acquire the writer's quality of mirth by a kind of "genetic osmosis". Mother was never too orthodox in matters of genetics. When I argued with Uncle Mel, she cautioned me to be more respectful. "Blood is thicker than water," she would pronounce.

"What blood, Mom? Mel is *your sister*'s husband!"

"That's exactly what I'm saying, Morris. Blood is thicker than water."

My father's adulation of the humorist's writings—we had several sets of the complete works of Sholom Aleichem and half a dozen biographies—was more related to his literary taste than to his sense of the absurd. Dad could never tell a story well. He was an old-world puritan. The word, sex, never crossed his lips in the presence of his children, and, if any of us spelled it out, he would blush. His naivete in such matters once manifested itself at the dinner table. My father had just returned from a convention of insurance agents in Banff, the Canadian Rockies, and he repeated an off-color story he had heard—without realizing its double-entendre implications.

Mother was taken off-guard. "Dushka!" (her pet name

for David—the Russian word for 'darling') "You should
be ashamed. In front of the children?" Dad's red hair
seemed to turn into flaming crimson.

Mother was the earthy one, and Dad the ethereal one
in our family. He would not have appreciated Sholom
Aleichem's irreverent way of playing with sacred texts.
The author's character, Tevyeh, loved to quote the Bible,
the prayer book, the wisdom of the ancient sages, and
then add an impish commentary. Tevyeh, for example,
would soliloquize about the fragility of life.

"Adam y'sodo me-ofor." ("Man's origin is dust, and
unto dust doth he return.") "In the meantime, a glass of
whiskey doesn't hurt!"

That didn't sound a bit like my teetotalling father.

Some years ago, on a Friday evening, I spoke in my
pulpit about "My Favorite Author". I depicted some
scenes from Sholom Aleichem's writings, and concen-
trated on the character of Tevyeh, the dairyman, hapless
parent of five daughters. One of the Temple officers, who
had been sitting near the altar at my side, reacted with
amazement. As we walked off the pulpit, he said,

"What a remarkable coincidence! I've just come back
from Detroit where I saw a preview of a new musical
based on the life of Tevyeh. Our music publishing company is doing the score, and it's terrific."

I told Bob that I had grave doubts about the success of
any story connected with Sholom Aleichem. The last
play I attended attracted an audience of less than two
hundred.

"This is different, rabbi. I'm sure of it."

"What's the play called?"

"Fiddler On the Roof."

"Are you kidding? What a bizarre title! It'll never
sell."

*　*　*

I have inherited my father's love of Yiddish. Three
people have a special place in my heart because of what
they have done to sustain the fresh vitality of the Yiddish
language for Jew and non-Jew alike: Maurice Samuel,
Isaac Bashevis Singer and, recently, Leo Rosten. It was
the filter of Samuel's incandescent mind and pen that
made possible the creation of *Fiddler On the Roof.*

Maurice Samuel described Yiddish as "a language of
refuge, intimacy, domesticity and affection." "It is a be-
nign, non-combative tongue, born of being on the losing
side of thousands of battles." A poet once said that a
language is the mirror of a people's soul. If you listen to
the 'music' of a language, you get its feeling tone, its
value system. When you soak an idea in thousands of
years of continuous living, there emerges a value, a
word, a phrase, that has a unique quality of its own.

Leo Rosten quotes Sholom Aleichem thirty-five times
in his masterful and memorable *Joys of Yiddish.* He writes
that the most characteristic quality of the language is its
irrepressibility. I can think of one incident that perfectly
documents Rosten's thesis.

During the American presidential campaign of 1936,
listeners to a program on a New York Yiddish-language
station heard the following announcement:

"My dear friends, I would like you to vote for Wendell
Willkie. Willkie is an honest man, a trustworthy man, a
gentleman. He is generous, unselfish. He loves Jews.
Truly a great human being." (Then, a brief pause) "This
is a paid political advertisement. I, personally, intend to
vote for Roosevelt."

Never Use Your Best French

I told my cousin that he had made a serious blunder. He was complaining about the embarrassment and humiliation he had suffered at the hands of the Paris police.

"You should have obeyed one of the first rules of tourist travel." I quoted the words of advice which foreign correspondent Walter Duranty had written a generation ago in his book "I write As I Please." Describing his difficulties in covering the Moscow scene, Duranty recommended that "whenever you are in trouble in a foreign country, speak in your own language—and speak louder."

Fred still felt the sting of his Paris tribulations.

"On our way to Paris from Spain, I bought a pair of sun-glasses at the Madrid airport. The style was a lot different from the ones we use here. When we arrived at the Paris hotel, it was late in the afternoon. We registered, and I handed over our passports to the desk clerk. I wanted to go right to our room, but you know my wife. Fran has a thing about gloves. Whenever we travel, she has to look for gloves.

" 'The stores will be closed soon, Fred. Let's send the baggage up to our room, and we'll take a little walk.' A few blocks from our hotel, Fran saw the sign, *Ganterie*. She asked me to wait outside; she would be out in a couple of minutes.

"I stood on the boulevard for awhile. A man stopped and asked me if I wanted to buy any postcards. I told him I wasn't interested—in French. You know, I speak French well. Then, he suggested that perhaps I had some foreign money to sell—*marché noir*. I kept telling him to get moving. He pleaded with me, I have five children to support, and a sick wife.

"I was handing him a franc when I felt a heavy hand on my shoulder. A French gendarme. '*Eh bien, monsieur*. The game is up. We know you Spanish . . .'

"What Spanish . . . ? I lifted my hand and felt my Madrid glasses.

"In my best French, I told the gendarme that I was an American. He was not surprised when I put my hand in my pocket and produced nothing. The gendarme ordered the two of us to accompany him to the police station. I pleaded that my poor wife can't speak French; she probably doesn't even know the name of our hotel. At least, let me step into the store.

"He let me know what he thought of my Spanish subterfuge, and the three of us walked down the boulevard. I kept looking at my watch. 'Poor Fran,' She will have a heart attack.

"The police officer at the gendarmerie was a lot smarter. After a few explanations, he released me. I ran outside to catch a taxi back to the boulevard. My God! It was a one-way street, the wrong way. So, I sprinted up the five long Parisian blocks, all the while looking at my watch. Forty-five minutes, and Fran was nowhere in sight.

"I entered the store, and there was Fran, calmly trying on gloves. She glowered at me.

"I can't understand you, Fred. You look a mess. What's wrong? I leave you outside for a couple of minutes. How come you're out of breath?' "

Rendezvous in Paris

In Confirmation Class, one of the tenth-graders will ask me, "Rabbi. have you ever read anything by Oscar Wilde?"

It was Wilde who once remarked that he never yielded to anything but temptation. My first impulse is to pin back the student's ears. But the memory of "the sins of my youth" restores my perspective.

The year was 1935. I had been ordained almost a year before when I attended a dinner at the University of Illinois Faculty Club. Seated next to me at the dais were an older couple, Professor and Mrs. Simon Littman. Dr. Littman was a nationally known economist. head of his department, and consultant to several cabinet members in the Roosevelt administration. Somehow the conversation turned to the subject of French Jewry, and I blithely asked the couple if they had ever heard of Captain Alfred Dreyfus. "You know, he was the French Jewish officer who was sentenced to Devil's Island on a false charge of treason, back in the 19th century."

The genial professor smiled at his wife.

"Captain Dreyfus? That's how we met!"

In 1897, a youthful graduate student at the University of Sorbonne was sitting at a sidewalk cafe in Paris. At the next table, two girls, recently graduated from the Uni-

versity of California, had arrived that day, about to make
le Grand Tour of Europe. One of the girls held a newspaper in her hand and read aloud the huge headline:
EMILE ZOLA, ATTORNEY SHOUTS: J'ACCUSE.

"I can't believe that anyone would have the nerve to
call the French military high command liars."

Simon Littman broke into their conversation. "It's
true. I just came from the trial. I heard Dreyfus defender
scream out the words, "J'accuse."

The professor told me that their sidewalk conversation led to a summer-long pursuit. He followed the girls
all through Europe, and in a St. Petersburg restaurant
proposed to the woman who was seated at my left.

Algiers Episode

Almost all the way across the Atlantic, flying in an Air Force C-54 from Washington to Casablanca, Marvin and I buried our noses in army foreign language manuals. Somehow Marvin had never studied French, and I was trying to master Arab colloquialisms that were not included in my classical Arabic courses. The time: March 4, 1944.

Marvin and I were the only chaplains on the plane, both of us, rabbis. Our orders read to report to U.S. Army Headquarters in Algiers.

In time of war the first day on an overseas assignment is unnerving, and we learned on Orders of the Day that Nazi planes had staged intermittent raids over Algiers. Army vehicles driven after sunset were restricted to the use of "cat's eyes" headlights, a thin slit of illumination. It was still light, though, when the two of us entered the Red Cross Officers' Club not far from the main Boulevard of the Algerian capital, but we stayed for only a few minutes because we planned to return to our quarters while we could still find our way in the unfamiliar African city.

In front of the Club, I heard a girl's angry cry. A cluster of people, gathered at the door, were staring at a young woman sitting on the sidewalk, her feet in the gutter. She was evidently shouting at three American lieutenants entering the Club. At the same time she was fighting off a few Arab street children who were tugging at her, begging for coins.

"*Chiens! Diables! Yallah lmshee!*" she cursed the youngsters.

Marvin pressed me to move away from the Club, but her last words struck my ears, "—*parce que je suis juive!*"

"What's she saying, Morris?"

"Marvin, we ought to find out what's bothering her. She's complaining that she's being mistreated because she's Jewish."

"Let's get going."

"At least, we ought to find out what's the problem."

I leaned down and we both lifted her from the gutter, and asked her if she lived nearby.

"*Pas loin d'ici.*" (Not too far.)

"We'll get you out of here."

By the time we reached the boulevard, I realized that I had made a mistake. She leaned heavily on both of us and wailed that the officers, after spending some time with her, had refused to take her into the Club. She continued to lean heavily on both of us, and I whispered to Marvin that I should have listened to him.

She turned her face toward Marvin, and gestured to him to get rid of me. How would he like some "eau de vie"—a little cognac?

"What's she saying?"

"We're in trouble, Marvin."

We reached the Boulevard and the swift darkness of the tropics enveloped the city. Only the dim lights of a long army convoy fell on us.

"Mademoiselle, we are American army chaplains. Rabbins. Aumoniers. Rabbis. Chaplains."

Obviously my French wasn't getting through to her;

she beckoned to me to jettison Marvin.

More slowly, I explained who we were. *Juives. Rabbins.*
"Ah!" the mists suddenly evaporated, *"Shema yisroel.
Mon Dieu."*

We were still on the Boulevard when she burst into a
Hebrew dirge. "Tzion Tamati. Tzion chemdati. . . ." I
hadn't heard that song since I was ten years old in Hebrew School. Her singing grew louder and more plaintive. I pulled up the lapels of my raincoat to cover the
Ten Commandments of my chaplain's insignia.

The rest of the way home—home was in the Casbah,
off-limits to military personnel, but neither of us knew
where the Casbah was—she poured out her life story.
She was born on the Isle of Rhodes. Her father was a
leading merchant. When the Nazis seized the Greek island, some officers brought her to Naples, where she
took to the streets. Somehow she made her way to North
Africa.

Marvin breathed a sigh of relief when we reached the
front door of her shabby hotel. He didn't have to tell me
what he thought of my judgment.

I almost forgot the episode in the pressure of work,
and Marvin diplomatically never referred to it again. A
week later, I was walking downhill on a street leading to
the Officers' Mess on my way to breakfast. Half a step in
front of me was a brigadier-general, headed in the same
direction toward his own Mess. Both of us stopped to
watch an army truck, filled with American soldiers evidently from forward lines. They were shouting at some
one across the street.

"Hey, Suzette. Climb aboard. C'mon, Suzette. Jump
up, Suzette."

The general and I could not see the object of their
attention. A traffic light changed. The khaki-green truck
moved on, and Suzette came into view. She was dressed

in a tight-fitting, bright-crimson silk dress. Her face was heavily rouged and her eyes darkened with thick Oriental mascara.

She caught a glimpse of me and her face broke into a broad smile of recognition. The general's chin dropped as she waved at me:

"Sholom aleichem, mon cher rabbin—God's peace be with you, my dear rabbi!"

What Our Synagogue
Needs Most

A French monsignor L'Hote wrote a book about fifty-two saints, almost all of them imaginary. Each of the saints had one specialty. One of them, St. Zephir, was gifted with the ability to convert nonbelievers while they lay asleep. "He approached their bed on tiptoe, knelt beside them and read in a low voice passages from Holy Scripture. Very soon the sleepers would begin to snore in a more harmonious fashion, a sure sign that in their dreams they were already visiting the green pasturse of Paradise."

The modern preacher, Christian or Jewish, finds it easy to identify with the mythical St. Zephir, plying his task among the sleepers. A rabbi is particularly challenged because most of his sermons are delivered to a Friday evening congregation, weary and heavy-lidded from the day's labors at week's end, and burdened down by an abundant traditional Sabbath repast.

Rabbi Murray Grauer observed one of his members bordering on a pleasant state of somnolence almost as soon as the Sabbath eve worship began. The rabbi wondered what would happen during the course of the sermon. As he started to preach, Rabbi Grauer observed his congregant-friend swaying back and forth, periodically pulling himself back from slumber. At the sermon's midway point, the man's body pendulum moved in an ever-growing arc—and the transfixed rabbi watched his parishioner fall forward to the floor with an ear-shattering —and sermon-shattering—thud.

The service ended and Rabbi Grauer stood in the receiving line, speculating on what the embarrassed congregant would say by way of apology.

"Rabbi," the awakened sleeper confidently announced as he shook the preacher's hand, "do you know what our synagogue needs most? Some good seat belts."

Once Over, Lightly

Once a year, in the early fall, my friend Weill visited New York during his buying season. Often, his stay in the metropolis coincided with the Jewish High Holyday season. For the past two years, one of his business hosts invited him to join his family at a synagogue on upper Lexington Avenue.

As they walked out of the synagogue, following Rosh Hashanah services, Weill remarked to his friend:

"Something struck me very odd. Your rabbi, Dr. Hyamson, gave that sermon last year. Seems to me it was word for word the same."

His host laughed. "There is more to that than you realize. Our rabbi, Moses Hyamson, is a great scholar, a professor at the Seminary. But, we have been trying unsuccessfully to have him retire since he was in his early seventies. He loves preaching, and he just won't listen to any talk of retirement, even in his eighties.

"Last Rosh Hashanah, after we heard the identical sermon five years running, we decided to do something about it. Our Board appointed a committee of men to meet with our revered spiritual leader. and to suggest, in as tactful a manner as possible, that he give a new message next year.

"Our committee was really diplomatic. In fact, they

decided not to pursue the matter in haste. Rather than offend the rabbi, they waited until after Chanukah, late in December, before they arranged an appointment.

"They met in the rabbi's home. He greeted his members in his usual warm, cherubic fashion, blessed them, and inquired about the nature of their mission. They stalled for quite a while, then, the chairman came right out with it: "Rabbi, I wonder if you realize that you have given the same Rosh Hashanah sermon for five years.

'Five years? You mean to say that I gave the same sermon five years? M . . . mn . . . what did I say?'

"The four men were caught off-guard. Not one of them could recall a single word of the rabbi's message.

"I guess you are right, gentlemen. I should preach a new sermon. But, just to make sure that I fix it in your minds, I will preach the old sermon once more next year!' "

Interrogatory Chess-game

An ancient Jewish tradition demands that you answer a question with a question. But then there is a problem: how do you terminate this interrogatory chess game? The answer: by asking an unanswerable question.

For example, consider the following scenario:

The place: In front of Temple Israelitico, Rome.
The time: The first week in June, 1944, the week of Liberation.

A Polish soldier approached me. He recognized the insignia on my uniform as that of a Jewish chaplain.

"Rabbi, do you know Goldstein of New York?"

"Do you know *Cohen* of Poland?"

"What is he—single or married?"

Check-mate in just two moves.

The Title Is the Message

The Seminary students were comparing notes during the Sunday night supper at the dormitory. They had returned from their week-end pulpits in New Jersey, Connecticut and New York, and each had a story to tell.

"Every week, I have the same problem. A reporter for the Hackensack Record calls me on Monday morning for my sermon title. Who knows what I'm going to talk about next Friday?"

A seminary dormitory is an ideal breeding-ground for practical jokers. Jules, our most perennial prankster, placed a call the following morning.

"This is Rabbi Kagan speaking. I want to give you my sermon title. Next Friday evening, I will speak on 'After This—What?' "

Kagan returned the following Sunday night with a euphoric look.

"You won't believe this. Every single seat was filled. I don't know why. I guess I'm really catching on in Hackensack!"

The next day, the Hackensack Record received a call with the following information:

"Rabbi Kagan will deliver a sequel to last week's sermon. He will preach on, 'After What—This?' "

The following Friday evening, there was a 'standing-room only' congregation in Hackensack.

Perils of the Speaker's Platform

Among the hazards which speakers on the banquet circuit have to face is the inept chairman, equipped with a bottomless store of malapropisms, and the master of ceremonies, whose pointless stories carry the event far into the night.

Sometimes the chairman simply has not yet mastered basic English. One of my colleagues had the unenviable experience of serving as a last-minute substitute for the renowned Dr. Stephen S. Wise. A substitute dreads to look out on the faces of a disappointed audience.

The chairman of the small-town Pennsylvania meeting waxed eloquent, as he expatiated on the historic achievements of the scheduled speaker whom illness had detained.

"Unfortunately, however, ladies and gentlemen, Rabbi Vise couldn't come. But I'm happy to present his very able prostitute."

Or the not-too-bright chairman. I attended a banquet in New Orleans, and listened to a lengthy introduction of an eloquent rabbi, Dr. Louis Binstock. After documenting the speaker's fame throughout the South, the chairman presented the learned rabbi. Dr. Binstock began, "Your generous introduction reminds me of the story of the old maid who was asked by her pastor if there was any truth to the story that she was engaged to be married. 'No, it's not true. It's only a rumor, but thank God for the rumor.' "

The following month, I was introduced to a Birmingham meeting by a man who had apparently attended the same New Orleans Conference. He recited an elaborate account of my background and assured his listeners that the speaker was famed all through the South. All of which reminded him of the story of the old maid. "It's not true. It's only a rumor. But thank God for the rumor."

Many years later, I addressed a service club in the Bronx. The program chairman presented my credentials, and ended with these words: "You men may not realize it, but Brother Morris is really quite famous. He's known from one end of the Bronx to the other."

I often wished that I had Maurice Samuel's skill in mastering the perfect retort. Samuel was a brilliant speaker, probably the most intellectually stimulating Jewish lecturer of the century. But he was ruthlessly candid with his audiences, and did not "suffer fools gladly." I recall his telling a Midwest audience, during the question period, to go home to bed. "You're already asleep mentally." But he saved his razor-edged barbs for heavy-handed chairmen. In Johannesburg, South Africa, he was introduced to a large gathering only a few hours after he had emerged from an arduous prop-plane flight from Europe. The chairman, Rabbi Rome, spent over forty minutes in a wearying introduction. The author rose, and in a withering voice declared, "Ladies and gentlemen, while Rome was fiddling, I was burning."

Eddie Cantor's quip, when he was presented after fourteen previous dinner speakers, struck a responsive chord in me, "My dear friends, when I came here, I was a young man!"

One of the most popular speakers of the 1940's and

1950's was the Dutch-American journalist, Pierre Van Paasen, a Christian lover of Zion. After the publication of his best-selling *Days of Our Years*, he was the most sought-after attraction on the Jewish lecture-circuit. Van Paasen told me of a recent harrowing experience.

The scene was a New Jersey B'nai Brith convention. After the long drawn-out dinner, he fidgeted for several hours, listening to greetings by the Governor, the Mayor, and a string of Lodge officers. Then came the presentation of plaques and the inevitable rambling speeches of acceptance. Van Paasen looked at his watch, 10:50 PM. The dauntless master of ceremonies announced:

"Before we hear from our guest speaker, may we introduce our distinguished friend, Mr. Abe Cahan."

The octogenarian journalist was the dean of Jewish letters, editor of the influential Jewish Daily Forward, and author of the most authentic portrayal of the early days of the New York Jewish ghetto, "The Rise of David Levinsky". Abraham Cahan was more than a literary figure: he was a monument before whom the audience arose and applauded for several minutes. The 82 year old Cahan rose and bowed. Then, to the guest speaker's horror, he yielded to an impulse to reminisce about his sixty years of public life. He did not return to his seat until five minutes past midnight! As he passed Van Paasen's chair, the about-to-be-introduced journalist touched his sleeve, and whispered, with all the sarcasm at his command, "Mr. Cahan, what made you stop?" The old man beamed with an appreciative grin, "Ah, you noticed, Mr. Van Paasen? My voice was still good, but my feet gave out."

The Orator

Oratory is one of the lost arts of the latter part of our century. The ancient Greeks, we know, valued the "rhetorical artist" as a prized member of society. Even though Aristotle was suspicious of men who were able to sway audiences by playing upon emotions and by a variety of verbal artifices, he acknowledged that oratory was a legitimate means of persuading large masses of people.

In our time, we are probably witnesses to the demise of oratory as an effective instrument of communication. My contemporaries remember Winston Churchill and Franklin D. Roosevelt and de Gaulle in the political arena. On a lower level, I can recall the two Bankhead brothers of Alabama, one a United States Senator, the other, Speaker of the House of Representatives. Both were orators whose mellifluous style was garnished with frequent allusions to the Bible, Shakespeare, Carlyle and Emerson.

Perhaps oratory disappeared the day when audiences were no longer at home in the world of Carlyle and Emerson. A famous 18th century clergyman once observed that "great preachers are made by great congregations."

Jews who are my contemporaries were fortunate in

spending the early years of their lives in the heroic Age of Jewish Oratory. My father and his generation regarded an eloquent speech as an object of veneration: an orator as a kind of shrine to be visited not only by adults but by children as well.

As a youngster in Toronto, I was brought up by parents to hear all the Jewish spell-binders who visited Canada. Chaim Weizmann, Schmarya Levin, Menachem Ussishkin, Rabbi Wolf Gold and our local gifted pulpiteer, Rabbi Barnett Brickner. We children were transfixed by their words and gestures, even if we could not follow their logic (Aristotle's first ingredient of oratory), nor could we fully comprehend their words. Often, the tone alone was sufficient to stir us profoundly. Rabbi Wolf Gold addressed a capacity crowd in Massey Hall at a rally on behalf of some Zionist cause. His full, jet-black beard, falling on long, vertical lines, gave him the appearance of an ancient Assyrian monarch. (Nebuchadnezzar surely must have looked like that!) Gold's basso-profundo voice was at least an octave below that of the operatic Chaliapin. The first five words fell from his lips in slow cadence that consumed most of the first minute. We balcony sitters almost fell out of our seats while we hung on each word that made the chandeliers shiver: "The—Jewish—people—lives—forever!"

The ideas were not particularly novel. They were refrains as familiar as a national anthem. Most speeches, the psychologist, Bonaro Overstreet, explained, are more in the nature of a ritual than an intellectual exercise. Those rituals of my childhood days were at least of ninety minutes duration. No speaker ever rose to the podium for less than an hour and a half.

The basic ingredient in the orator's make-up, it seems to me, is a feeling of his own greatness. He senses, in the words of Carlyle, the heroic quality within himself. He does not engage in conversation; he holds court. To call it vanity is somehow to miss the point. It's like calling St. Francis an egotist because he confided to his teen-age peers: "You will see that some day I shall be adored by all the world." Perhaps the French *hauteur* catches some of the essence of it.

Physical appearance was invariably an element in the orator's equipment. Just to look at Rabbi Stephen S. Wise or Rabbi Abba Hillel Silver was enough to transform those present into expectant listeners. I believe it was Eleanor Roosevelt who said that a person at forty has the face he deserves. Both Wise and Silver were tall, broad-shouldered; their heads much larger than average, almost leonine, and their long hair was generally so unruly that they frequently paused to run their fingers through their impressive locks—a highly dramatic act in itself.

Paradoxically, the Age of the Microphone has not enhanced the spellbinder's art. Dr. Wise never made peace with the technology of amplification. He waved aside the microphone as he stood before a Madison Square Garden audience of 18,000 gathered for a Zionist rally. If John Wesley's voice could reach the ears of tens of thousands gathered in a Yorkshire or Georgia valley, before the days of loud-speakers, why did his powerful voice require mechanical boosting?

At one such rally, the crowd assembled to hear Dr. Wise's arguments against the proposal to partition Palestine. Some of Wise's European colleagues, the Zionist leaders of the Continent, supported acceptance of Great Britain's partition plan, offering part of the Holy Land to the Arabs, part to the Jews. Not so Rabbi Wise. In a single word, he swept aside all our doubts as he shouted the thunderous challenge: "This is not par—ti—tion. This is an am—pu—ta—tion.' As he spoke, he swept his huge hands sharply in front of his knees, and we had the feeling that he had just split us in two!

In a television program which I moderated, I once asked Robert St. John, biographer of many of the world's leaders, how he would identify greatness. He suggested this simple test: "If you are in a room with a large number of people, with your back to the door, and a great person enters, if you *feel* a *presence*, that is greatness."

As I suggested earlier, the great person himself must sense that presence within his being. When I taught at the University of Iowa, we invited Dr. Wise to address our Sunday Night Vesper Service. As we awaited his arrival at the Rock Island railroad station, the Head of the School of Religion, Dr. Willard Lampe, recounted a previous experience with the eminent preacher. Several years before, Rabbi Wise was invited to be the Vespers speaker. He arrived on the late afternoon train that Sunday. As the "Rock Island" was approaching Iowa City, the rabbi peered out of the car window and watched a heavy rainstorm pounding against the pane. He wondered if there would be any audience by 8 o'clock. Indeed, would there be any one at the station to meet him? The train entered the station, and Dr. Wise, suitcase in hand, donned his black fedora, an impressive broad-brimmed hat that had become a kind of Wise trademark. From the car platform, he was amazed to see a tremendous crowd of students, professors and townspeople standing in the drenching rain. Unknown to him, the passengers in the car ahead were the Iowa football team, returning from New Haven. Underdogs all season, they had scored an upset victory over a brilliant Yale team. The hero of the hour was All-American Aubrey Devine, who had scored Iowa's winning touchdown. A band played and the throng shouted in rhythmic unison: "Yea, Devine! Yea, Devine!"

The Jewish divine from Manhattan raised his black fedora in a proud wave of acknowledgement to the rain-soaked welcoming assemblage.

*   *   *

My wife and I, in the summer of 1936, were privileged to enjoy the companionship of Jewry's most popular Yiddish orator, Rabbi Zvi Hirsch Masliansky, the world-famous preacher of New York's Lower East Side. Masliansky possessed that "presence" delineated by Robert St. John: a white patriarchal beard, an erect posture even in his 81st year, cheeks reflecting an uncommon vigor, and a strong voice which lost none of its resonance in old age. The Maslianskys and we occupied adjoining rooms in a Tel Aviv hotel. Arab riots had broken out that summer, and the elderly couple rarely moved away from the hotel porch and gardens.

Our neighbor "adopted" us, and delivered speeches to us that reminded us of Disraeli's quip about his Prime Minister opponent, "Gladstone addresses Queen Victoria as if she were the House of Parliament." Masliansky never conversed: he declaimed, he soliloquized, he held forth, but he never spoke.

The veteran rabbi's oratory was often directed toward my wife. She was almost sixty years his junior. As they sat in the garden, he told her, "You are the bright sunrise! I am the fading shadows of sunset! You are the fresh breath of Spring! I, the falling leaves of autumn." Mrs. Masliansky, rocking on the porch chair, would remonstrate with her husband.

"Zvi Hirsch, stop talking that way. You make me sound so ancient!" (She was five years his junior.)

The preacher turned toward the porch, and with a Gladstone-Queen Victoria flourish, waved his hand in a gallant sweep, and boomed out: "Ah, my love, my darling, *dos is die tragedia in unser leben.* . . . that's the tragedy of our lives. An old man like me mated to a beautiful young girl like you!"

We left them one day to make a hazardous bus trip to Jerusalem. Every few days, Arab snipers on the hair pin curves of the Judean hills, had killed or wounded bus drivers, and it was far from comforting to see two British soldiers strapped to the roof of our bus, fingers on machine guns. When we returned, Rabbi Masliansky greeted us with the question,

"Did you get to the top of Mount Scopus?" We reported our visit there, to see the beginnings of Hadassah hospital, and the Hebrew University. He had made the trip earlier in the year.

"Was it a clear day on Scopus?" It usually was not. "The day we went there," he mused, "the customary haze had vanished, and we could see all the way across the broad Jordan Valley, to hills that were thirty miles away. I gazed out at the distant mountains of Moab, to the spot where Master Moses stood when he beheld the Promised Land. There he was, standing on his mountain top, and I, on mine. We had a long conversation. I spoke to Moses our Master, and I could almost imagine his answers."

Moses was eighty years old when he stood at Mount Sinai in the wilderness: the Manhattan rabbi was eighty in that hour of spiritual confrontation. And he repeated what he had said to us in one of our earlier porch meetings.

"What a shame. Just when you have the clearest thoughts in all your life, you're no longer able to communicate them to the world!"

The One and the Many

The Jewish ban against polygamy is, relatively, not very old. In a religious law promulgated almost a thousand years ago, Western Jews were interdicted against taking more than one wife. But, even in recent years, Jews living in the Moslem world, numbering many hundreds of thousands, leaned on the biblical warrant for multiple wives. In very early medieval times, the limit was set at four, and this influenced Moslem law as well. Jews, living in North Africa, Yemen, Iraq and Syria, in turn, followed their Moslem hosts in accepting a maximum of four wives. Only when the State of Israel was declared, in 1948, and Jewish immigrants from Arab lands poured into the new State, was polygamy finally abolished.

One of our Seminary professors, Dr. Louis Ginzberg, the world's foremost authority on the Talmud, married in his late thirties. His wife, Adele, at the time of their marriage, was in her very early twenties. After they had been married for twenty years—at the time I met them —she retained the fresh blonde beauty of her youthful days.

In 1933, our professor returned from a sabbatical semester of teaching at the newly-founded Hebrew University in Jerusalem. He described their visit to an Oriental rabbi in the Holy City. At sixty, Dr. Ginzberg's white beard added years to his appearance. On the other hand, his wife, in her early forties, looked ten years younger than her age. At the Sabbath dinner table, the host rabbi glanced at the professor's wife, and murmured to his guest:

"What a clever fellow you are! You left the old one back in New York."

As the Talmud Says: All Beginnings Are Difficult

Deep in the heart of New Jersey, some fifty years ago, a synagogue was established by the pioneer Jews who had settled in a new community. As time passed, they purchased a building for worship and for the religious nurture of their children. But they lacked a cemetery of their own. Traditionally, a Jewish congregation acquires "holy ground" (the religious term for a Jewish burial area) almost from the moment of its inception. The first Jews who landed in New Amsterdam in 1654 made certain, in that very year, that "holy ground" would be procured at the same time that facilities for worship were found.

The New Jersey synagogue elders recognized their oversight when the inevitable happened. Older members of the community passed away, and their loved ones made the journey to Staten Island or Brooklyn to bury their dead. The congregational officers determined that they would establish their own cemetery. Two acres of farmland were bought, on the rim of the town, and now they were a full-fledged synagogue.

Two years passed without incident. Then the mother of one of their board members died, and the moment arrived for the cemetery to be used for the first time. The family of the deceased, however, could not bring themselves to leave their dear one resting all alone in the new holy grounds. Graveside services were held in Brooklyn. A second congregational loss produced the same problem. No one wanted to leave his beloved kinsman in isolation.

A special Board meeting was called to consider how to break the impasse. After hours of frenetic discussion, one member had a brilliant inspiration. Why not appoint a committee, consisting of three of their leading citizens, an attorney, a physician and an accountant, to produce a candidate for the long-empty cemetery?

A few days later, three men appeared in the office of the Superintendent of a Jewish Home for the Aged in New York City, and presented a rather unique request. Could he suggest the name of one of the residents who might fulfill the following three requirements:

a) That person would have no living relatives, and

b) have no financial means, and (most important of all)

c) not be in good physical health?

Puzzled by such a strange request, the Superintendent, nevertheless, mentioned an old-timer by the name of Shlomo. Shlomo was far from the oldest in the institution—he was seventy-eight—but he was alone in the world, never received guests, was penniless, and had a syndrome of ailments, each of which might be regarded as terminal.

The Committee, after proper introductions, presented a document to Shlomo, and explained.

"You should only live till one hundred and twenty. If you sign here, you will be given a free burial. And, for the rest of your life, you will receive twenty-five dollars a week." (A prodigious sum in those days.)

The Committee, combining the wisdom of three disciplines, law, medicine and accounting, calculated that the agreement would cost the congregation not more than one hundred dollars. And their stratagem had the added merit of performing a good deed for a deserving resident of the Home for the Aged.

Shlomo examined the legal papers perfunctorily, and without hesitation signed three copies.

Several months passed, and not a word reached the Committee of Three. They phoned the Superintendent and solicitously inquired about Shlomo's health.

"I'm sorry. I really can't tell you. We lost Shlomo. Yesterday, he moved into his own apartment."

Some time later, the frantic committee had to report that Shlomo had made a down payment on a small grocery store—in New Jersey. Twenty-five dollars a week was more than enough for his modest needs.

By year's end, the shame-faced Committee announced to the Board that Shlomo had taken on a wife, and the two of them were managing their thriving grocery store. In the meantime, the Synagogue cemetery problem remained unsolved.

*   *   *

I wish I knew the details of subsequent events. That is all I heard from a New Jersey friend. I imagine that, like all cemeteries, the New Jersey one ultimately began to take in members of the Synagogue. What happened to Shlomo apparently is lost to history. Conceivably, his grocery store was absorbed by a giant conglomerate, and he is now one of its vice-presidents.

Old Man Glassman

Old Man Glassman, a pillar of the tiny synagogue of Iowa City, had his troubles every December. Even in his late eighties he would ride horseback, a familiar figure in the campus town. Believe it or not, Old Man Glassman's problems came from the community's very young children. Since he had a ruddy complexion, burnished red by the sharp winds of many Iowa winters, and a full snow-white beard that was more authentically Santa Claus than any department store impostor's, youngsters pursued him, shouting their Christmas requests. It was a little embarrassing for a pious Jew who wrapped himself in his prayer shawl every morning, both at home and in the Synagogue.

I was with Old Man Glassman when he left this world in his eighty-ninth year. So often death comes with indignity, but not for Glassman with the cherubic face. His breathing was not labored as he lay on the hospital bed, his patriarchal face serene and without a trace of pain. When the breathing stopped, I understood the meaning of the ancient rabbinic legend about Moses dying with "the kiss of God."

A few months before his death, Glassman sat by my side in the Iowa City Synagogue on the holiest day of the year, Yom Kippur. Traditionally, on the Day of Atone-

ment, observing Jews never left the House of God from
sunrise to sunset. But a crisis loomed for some of the
worshippers and their thoughts wandered to the neighboring football stadium where the annual game between
the University of Iowa and their traditional foes, the
Badgers of the University of Wisconsin, was about to
begin. And it was Homecoming Day, which summoned
all the loyal alumni.

By one-thirty in the afternoon of the sacred Day,
nearly half of the pews were empty, and Old Man Glassman kept muttering into his beard: "Where are they all
going?"

I whispered the news about the classic rivalry which
beckoned across the Iowa River.

"Heathens, heretics, pack of the ungodly!" he talked
into his beard throughout his afternoon prayers.

There was a pause in the service and his eyes flashed:
"Rabbi, do you know what I can't understand. Why
don't parents have more control over their children?"

"Mr. Glassman, maybe you didn't notice, but your son
is among the missing—a heathen of sixty-five—and your
grandson, Dr. Arthur, isn't here either!"

Till after four o'clock Old Man Glassman interspersed
his Yom Kippur benedictions with a few lamentations
about "America *Goniff*"—the New World which had
eroded some of the age-old loyalties.

As the autumnal sun began to set in the western Iowa
skies, the renegades began to stream in. My neighbor
rose from his East Wall seat and strode toward his grandson.

"Arthur, you *shaygetz* (unbeliever), you ought to be
ashamed. . . . Who won?"

"*Zaida*, (Grandpa) we won for a change. The Hawk-
eyes beat Wisconsin 19 to 7."

Old Man Glassman returned to my side, and the majestic *Neilah* service began—the Closing of the Gates of Supplication. Mingled with his prayers, the patriarch mumbled into his beard, which had somehow acquired a beatific look: "Imagine that! 19 to 7. We won, 19 to 7."

Aunt Tess

When a clergyman does research in preparation for a eulogy at a funeral, there are many pitfalls. Sometimes he has to rely completely on the emotion-laden descriptions of the nearest of kin, and the picture that emerges at the service may be one that friends barely recognize.

One of our rabbinic stock-in-trade stories is about a family who had difficulty finding a rabbi who would bend the facts enough to disguise the truth about their ne'er do well husband and father. The rabbi who finally volunteered spoke these words at the graveside:

"Abe had a brother in Chicago who was thoroughly dishonest—a scoundrel. Compared to that brother, Abe was a saint!"

I hesitated when my friend Ned asked me to officiate at the funeral of his maiden aunt Tess. I had never met her.

"Ned, you say that she had three nieces and two nephews, including yourself. I'd like to meet them an hour before the service."

We gathered in a Bronx funeral home.

"What can we tell you about Tess? She was seventy-six years old, and we had to chip in for her support the last few years. We can't think of anything good about her. She was just a plain, selfish, petty old lady. The less you say, the better."

My eulogy was a judicious mixture of restrained generosity and a discreet avoidance of violating the commandment: Thou shalt bear no false witness.

At the graveside there were seven of us: the five mourners, the rabbi, and, seemingly emerging from nowhere, a very old man in a crumpled suit. His eyes were filled with tears, and he lingered over the grave as we left to go toward our cars.

"A relative?" I asked Ned.

"Never laid eyes on him."

How had he managed to reach the Westchester cemetery?

I held back to satisfy my curiosity and discovered that the old man had no way to return to his home in the Bronx except by using a number of busses.

We rode back in my car.

"How well did you know Tess?"

He broke into tears again, the tired tears of the aged.

"Rabbi, did you look at her in the coffin? What an angel! What a beauty! Do you know why she was so beautiful? Because she was that way inside. A living angel. I met her sitting on a bench on the Grand Concourse. Every day these past six years, when we could, we sat on the same bench and talked all day. Oy, a real angel. A beautiful soul. A young woman!"

As we neared his home, he asked me if I knew his nephew, Norman, a great rabbi. I told him that we were old friends.

Rabbi Norman and I happened to meet the following Sunday at a Synagogue Council meeting. I mentioned that I had met his uncle last Sunday.

"You're mistaken, Morris, You couldn't have."

We argued about it for a moment. "You must be wrong."

I persisted. "Did you say, last Sunday? You're right, Morris. He died last Monday."

The Arsonist

The ride to the other end of the city, to the Westville Mental Health Hospital was a long one. My friend, Judge Landsman, and I had an appointment with the Director of the Hospital, in connection with a community planning project. The judge talked about the complexities of mental health problems.

"I'll tell you a story, rabbi, which you may find incredible. Almost forty years ago, a young man, fresh from a teachers' college, found himself a position in a village school about fifty miles north of the capital. During the depression years, teaching positions were scarce, and doubly so for Jewish teachers.

The first week he was there, one of the local churches invited him to take over a Sunday School class. It was a village tradition. The new teacher explained apologetically that he was not a Christian. About a month later, the young man came to the School Board with a letter in his hand. He had received a scrawled message that there was no room for Jews in their village.

The Chairman suggested that he ignore the letter. Some time later, a second warning came, this time threatening him with bodily harm. Again, the young man was reassured by Board Members. "Pay no attention to crackpots. We like your work."

"Another month passed. An alarmed teacher appeared at the home of the School Board chairman. This time, the threat extended to the small school itself. If he did not leave town, the writer would burn down the school. A few days later, a midnight fire levelled the modest building.

"Since the United States mails were involved, federal authorities were called in to help the local police. Within a few weeks, they traced the author of the threatening messages. The three letters had been written by the teacher himself.

"At a conference of State and Federal law enforcement officials, the problem of jurisdiction arose. Arson was a State offense; threatening letters, sent through the mails, fell within the jurisdiction of the United States Attorney's office. The State attorney, a kind-hearted man, observed that the defendant had a serious emotional problem. If he were committed to a State Institution, it would be one with few psychiatric resources. Why not have him tried in Federal court? If the young teacher is found guilty, he happened to know that at a certain federal penal facility, there was an excellent psychiatrist in charge.

"In a United States court, the teacher received a sentence of several years, and soon found himself under the tutelage of a young psychiatrist who took a great deal of interest in his extraordinary patient."

The Judge reminded me that, in his younger days, he was a probation officer with the federal government.

"One day, I received a call from a warden with an unusual request. Could I help an about-to-be-released prisoner enter medical school? The young man, fully rehabilitated, had become enamored with the work of his psychiatrist. His ambition was to follow in the doctor's footsteps.

"Eight years later, he completed his residency in psychiatry, and promptly became an assistant to the man he worshipped. In the intervening years, his psychiatrist had left the government service, and was now head of a very large hospital."

As we neared our destination, I asked the judge if he had followed the career of his ward.

"Indeed. He ultimately succeeded his chief as Hospital Head, when the good man retired; he now has a national reputation as an authority on mental health!"

There Is No Word for "Privacy" in Yiddish

The problem was not a new one. It might be called, inter-marriage, Jewish style. How to resolve the conflict between an engaged couple both Jews, who were brought up in different branches of the faith? He was an attorney, reared in a religiously observant Orthodox home; she was a psychologist who had been exposed to what might be called a classic Reform tradition.

One afternoon, he pleaded with me to help them find a common meeting ground. They had battled all the last evening, and had wearily decided that tonight was the deadline. Either they discover some compromise, or the engagement was off.

I told him that their deadline did not fit into my plans for the evening. I wasn't free. He groaned with disappointment.

"It's tonight or we're through."

Harvey and Lola were not impulsive youngsters. He was thirty-five and his fiancée, twenty-nine.

Could I at least spare an hour for supper together? We agreed to meet at Steinberg's Dairy Restaurant on upper Broadway, a familiar eating place for westsiders. It was a rendezvous for Yiddish writers: at almost every lunch-hour, Isaac Bashevis Singer sat at one of the Steinberg tables. And, invariably, it was crowded.

Harvey suggested that I invite my wife to join us, but I demurred. His motive was not hospitality, nor the hope that she would share in the counselling situation. He simply wanted to make sure that we would have privacy in our booth, because Steinberg waiters did not regard an empty seat with favor.

Our discussion began as we ate supper, and, within a few moments, it grew heated. It was a case of the immovable versus the irresistible. Tradition stood its ground, and liberalism refused to budge.

Our waiter, as predicted, glowered at the empty seat and kept asking if we were expecting anyone. I half-nodded in the dim hope that he would interpret my answer to be affirmative. Then, muttering his exasperation, he escorted a tall, middle-aged man to our booth.

The couple's arguments were not cooled by the intrusion. Lola maintained that she was definitely not going to limit her kitchen to kosher food. She saw no sense in "those vestiges of primitive superstition." Harvey volunteered the thought that, at least, they try it for a couple of years.

As each one spoke, the stranger peered intently into the face of the protagonist, shaking his head in silent approval or disapproval. We lingered over dessert, as the two scored points. Our "guest" had finished, and held his check between his fingers, awaiting the outcome of the debate. He glanced at his watch, and half-rose from his seat.

"Young woman, do you want my opinion?"

She icily indicated that she didn't.

"Let me ask you something, my dear young lady. Will it hurt you to keep kosher? Will it kill you to keep kosher? It ain't poison!"

It was not likely that the seat would long remain vacant, and I suggested that they escort me a few blocks up

Broadway to the crosstown bus. The hour was late for my appointment. On the street, we would have some privacy.

As we neared 86th Street, the girl fell back on her training as a psychologist.

"Do you know, the more I think about it, the more I realize that I have some psychological block. To me, the word, kosher, makes me think of the lower East Side, of dirty stores and . . ."

At that moment, I felt a tap on my shoulder. A woman, walking behind us on Broadway, blurted out,

"Excuse me, mister. That's a very interesting question. Do you mind if I listen to your answer?"

Circumcision on Schedule

One of the culture conflicts which Jews experience is related to the problem of punctuality. The Anglo-Saxon world, into which most of them have entered in the course of the last century, regards time with a sense of precision that "the eternal people" have generally not taken too seriously. Hence, the expression, "Jewish time." (I have heard other minority groups use a comparable expression for their own indifference to punctuality.)

Of course, German and Austrian Jews have embraced the traditions of their Teutonic hosts. And third-generation Jews have absorbed the customs of the land. A three o'clock wedding means that the music will begin promptly at that hour. Eastern European Jews regard such pre-occupation with precision as "an imitation of the Gentiles."

The director of the Office of Israel's Chief Rabbinate, a Manchester Jew, told me of the difficulties he had encountered in organizing the funeral of the late Chief Rabbi the previous day. It was scheduled for noon, and all the Israeli officials and foreign diplomats were in their seats promptly at that hour. The rites began on time. A number of rabbis, particularly those who had to rush in from outside Jerusalem, all of them natives of Poland and Rumania, had vented their wrath upon him for the indignity: "Our Chief Rabbi has to have a Gentile funeral?"

On one occasion, I felt that the Anglo-Saxons and the Prussians were carrying things too far in structuring time.

The event was a Bris, a circumcision. The location: one of the most prestigious hospitals in Manhattan's East Side. It was operated more in the manner of a hotel than a hospital. Movie actresses spent two weeks there, on a diet program. Generals, business tycoons and heiresses luxuriated in its facilities. And it was very fastidious in its scheduling.

A circumcision schedule called for the following procedures:

10 A.M. The doctor and the baby (with nurse) arrive simultaneously in the small circumcision room. A clamp is placed on the infant.

10:07. The clamp is removed as the family and the rabbi, who was invited to name and bless the baby, enter. Surgery follows.

10:09. The rabbi names and blesses the baby. The infant is given a sip of sacramental wine.

10:12. A maid enters with a tray of cookies.

10:16. The room is cleared.

On this morning, the routine was threatened by an untoward development. During surgery, the great-uncle of the baby, a husky giant of a man, well over six feet, turned yellow, green and red, as he watched the surgeon, and slumped to the floor. His nephew, the six-foot-four father of the child, followed suit, forming a human letter L. The time: 10:11. I reached for the wine, as I leaned down and held up the father's head. He had not yet pronounced the "father's blessing". The doctor whispered, "Rabbi, wine's no good for that. We need whiskey."

As we spoke, the hour of 10:12 arrived. The door

opened. An attractive waitress, in a black and white uniform, walked in. Tray in hand, she looked straight ahead, gingerly stepped over one of the prostrate figures, then the other, and, in a sweet high-pitched voice, beckoned, "Have a cookie, please."

Stranger at the Funeral

For New Yorkers, a long strike which had deprived them of their New York Times was tantamount to a Siberian exile sentence. A good part of their lives was conducted in a state of suspended animation. Those who felt most deprived were the traditional Jewish families who suffered a loss. For there was virtually no opportunity to communicate information about the time and place of the funeral in the traditionally brief time between death and burial.

A close friend, faced with this problem, worried about the large number of friends who would not learn of her father's passing.

"Dad helped so many people over the years, I'm sure they would have wanted to pay their respects, if only they knew."

Esther's father, a prominent business man, was a member of an illustrious Hasidic family. Her uncle, his brother, was a world-famous Rebbe. As it turned out, the chapel was crowded with hundreds of friends and associates, many of them dressed in the traditional Hasidic garb.

Moving through the crowd, an old bearded man entered into the private mourners' parlor, telling the attendant, "I'm one of the mourners." As the family entered the mortuary limousine, the stranger whispered the same words to the chauffeur and sat in the middle seat. Esther surveyed him quizzically and asked her uncle who the man was. No answer came. The pious rabbi buried his head in a Book of Psalms which he recited quietly. There could be no external distraction.

At graveside, the prayers ended, and family members took turns with a shovel to place a bit of earth on the coffin.

The stranger edged his way forward, raised the shovel, declared again that he was one of the mourners, and joined in the farewell ritual.

During the seven days of mourning, Esther unsuccessfully tried to pry loose from her uncle some information about the intruder. He would not utter a word other than prayer.

At week's end, Esther came to me to pour out her outrage.

"My uncle finally explained it all to me, and it's much worse than I thought. The man really was an intruder, a total stranger. All the way to the cemetery, in the limousine, he kept leaning forward, praising my father for all the wonderful kindnesses he had done for him. He had helped this old man get his first job when he came to America. Obtained different employment for him when his boss wanted him to work on the Sabbath."

"My uncle laughed when he told me: the bearded old gentleman kept referring to his benefactor as Jake Millgram. Dad's name, as you know, was Samuels. At that busy chapel, there was another service which began at the same time, and the old man followed the wrong group of mourners."

I comforted Esther with an explanation that seemed to satisfy my friend.

"You told me, Esther, that the stranger was very striking in appearance. Perhaps a little unearthly. Among all those bearded Hasidim, he stood out. Several of your friends, especially your Christian friends, commented on the man's saintly demeanor. I wonder if it isn't related to the New York Times strike. Your generous father had done so much for a lot of people, all his life. So many of them weren't there to mourn with you. Possibly the mysterious stranger was the prophet Elijah, come to Manhattan. According to tradition he keeps coming back to earth for a variety of missions. Elijah may have been conveying *their* appreciation."

Esther smiled for the first time in a month.

"Perhaps, rabbi, perhaps."

"Jews Always"

On an Atlantic cruise, my wife and I entered a bridge tournament: on cruises, good sportsmanship takes precedence over sound judgment.

Our opponents were a couple from Fort Wayne, Indiana, and we mumbled introductions as we sat down for the first round. Our conversation was relaxed and congenial, despite the disparity in age. Julia and I were in our twenties, our Indiana opponents, middle-aged.

At one point in the game, I opened with a bid of one, no trump.

Mrs. S. lowered her cards momentarily, "It's a funny thing: Jews always bid, no trump."

Julia looked at me, her eyes asking if she should tell her. . . .

"Mrs. S., my husband and I are both Jewish."

Mr. S., his face beet-red, glared at his wife.

The Indiana matron was not taken aback. She lifted her cards and cheerily added:

"It's a funny thing. They bid no-trump—and they always make it."

Miracle of the Name

The doctor informed Mrs. Kress that there was little hope for her son Philip. He had been running a fever of over 106 for almost a week.

"We have no cure for spinal meningitis (this was in the mid-1930's), and the chance of his pulling through are less than one out of twenty. If he does make it, I am afraid that there may be permanent brain damage."

Mrs. Kress came to see me that Friday afternoon.

"Rabbi, at Sabbath services tonight, would you please change Philip's name?"

I had known of the tradition, a mystical belief, that one way to fool the Angel of Death was to alter the name of the person in danger. According to this Cabbalistic notion, the Messenger of Death was armed with a summons containing the name of his intended candidate. The only way to confuse him was to change the name of his projected victim.

At nine that evening, in the presence of my student congregation, we proceeded with the ritual. Philip Kress became Chayim Kress. Rather diffidently, I explained that "Chayim" meant *life*. The students were as skeptical as I was, but our prayers for Phil were heartfelt.

The next morning, I arrived at the hospital, and was greeted by a happy mother. Chayim's doctor broke the news:

"Last night, around nine o'clock, Philip's temperature broke, and went down to normal. I expect he'll have no after-effects.

Mrs. Kress pressed the physician's hand.

"The rabbi must have done what I asked him. He must have changed Philip's name."

Faith or Reason

At the dinner table, Judy was reporting some of the happenings in her Temple Confirmation Class for tenth-graders. In the after-glow of her experience, a little more than an hour before, she spoke with animation:

"Mom, if God has a face, it must look like Milton Steinberg."

Judy was talking about her teacher and family rabbi, the forty-four year old spiritual leader of a Manhattan congregation. Judy's rhapsodic outburst about their rabbi did not startle her parents. They shared her estimate of Rabbi Steinberg; her youthful exuberance had probably distilled very graphically their own adulation of the man.

As Dr. Steinberg's associate for a number of years, I was fascinated by this relationship between a large congregation in the heart of sophisticated and blasé upper East-Side Manhattan and their rabbi. Congregants rarely referred to him as Rabbi or Doctor Steinberg. It was simply Milton. Even the young people referred to him by his first name.

There are two kinds of familiarity: one, a reflection of intimacy, as in a family relationship; the other, born of hero-worship. In a paradoxical way, when we place a fellow human-being on a pedestal, we somehow put a great deal of emphasis on his first name; as if to say: his family name is an accident of birth; his given name represents his uniqueness. We stress *Albert* Einstein, *Winston* Churchill, *Jascha* Heifetz, *"Ike"* Eisenhower.

This observation may seem a little out-dated. The modern trend is toward a flippant, casual use of the first name, especially in the western part of the United States. An Arizona clergyman takes it for granted that he will be called Frank, or Jack, or Bill, within an hour after introduction.

Some of my contemporaries took themselves much more seriously. The wife of a rabbi I know used his title when she spoke of him or to him in the presence of others. "Will the rabbi have another cup of coffee?"

When her friends commented on her formality, she explained:

"My husband really thinks of himself as, Rabbi. He doesn't even call himself by his first name. When he shaves in the morning, the face he sees in the mirror is not Samuel, or Sam, or Sammie. He only sees Rabbi in the mirror."

Rabbinical narcissism, like its apposite number within the Christian clergy, is one of the hazards of a profession whose major activity is worship. Thomas Carlyle's classic essays on "Heroes and Hero Worship" begin with a study of "The Hero As Divinity". His familiar thesis that "hero worship is the foundation-stone of society" is based on the conviction that any one who worships God must be lost in admiration for the greatest of all God's creations—Man. "We touch heaven when we lay hand on a human body. . . . We are the miracle of miracles—the great inscrutable mystery of God."

The beauty of Milton Steinberg was that he seemed completely unaffected by the adulation poured upon him in his brief life-time. (He died at the age of forty-six.) He assumed that when a teen-ager called him Milton, it was out of a feeling of comradeship. It never dawned on him that the young person was really saying St. Milton.

The two qualities of the rabbi, which are most memorable to me, were intensity and love. How can one's eyes express that warmth and intensity? Even Milton's photographs, which still adorn many of his congregants' homes since his death in 1950, evince both qualities at the same time. An intense softness, a soft intensity. I sat next to him when he addressed a class of fourteen-year-olds. At the end of the hour, I noticed the palm of his right hand. There was a line of blood which had come through the skin from the pressure of his finger-nails.

Many people, of course, are loving human beings. Saintly love, if I may use an extravagant term, which would have been abhorrent to Milton Steinberg, is on a different level. The word, passion, does not capture it, because no element of sexuality is involved. Those who were touched by his life sensed that they were in the presence of a personage whose heart was a Niagara Falls of loving. It poured out endlessly, as if its possessor would burst if the love were dammed up within him.

Milton's capacity for love also had room for anger. He told his congregation that indignation was "one of the most honorable of human traits." Losing your temper was not in itself a sin. Moses, the noblest of men, vented his indignation on the worshippers of the Golden Calf. Of Jesus, the incarnation of pure love for Christians, tradition "could not keep a picture of him as moral unless it included indignation in his makeup."

What was unique about Milton Steinberg was the combination of a warm heart and a scintillating intellect. It was almost as if the inexhaustible energy within him flowed both to the heart and to the head at the same time. I am avoiding the temptation to dwell on his numerous books, all of them gems of English prose. It is rare for the beauty of a human being to shine through his literary creations.

How can a preacher be profound and excitingly popular at the same time? Even when Rabbi Steinberg preached about Love, as he did in an exquisite sermon entitled, "A Pity For the Living," the listener had to sit on the edge of his seat, alert to the subtleties of his discourse on gentleness and tenderness. On those occasions, when he expounded on such abstruse subjects as a Jewish view of Kierkegaard's existentialism, I watched the ecstatic faces of his listeners. They seemed to be saying: "I haven't the vaguest idea of what Milton is talking about, but isn't it beautiful? His thoughts are divine!"

Since his college days, Milton Steinberg was torn, like his 12th century idol, Moses Maimonides, between faith and reason. In his mid-teens, he was a student of the classics, far removed from Hebraic influences, and he worshipped at the shrine of Reason. Later, when he plunged into Jewish studies, his inspiration came from the rationalists, especially Mordecai M. Kaplan, the founder of the Reconstructionist movement. The God he discovered was "the Force in the universe that makes for righteousness," not a personal Deity Who supervised the individual actions of Man.

Only during the last few years of his life did Milton Steinberg search for answers beyond reason. Eight centuries before him, the greatest of all Jewish thinkers in history, Maimonides, reversed the procedure. The 12th century philosopher produced a classic credo, when he was twenty-three years old, beginning with the words, "I believe with a perfect faith. . . ." In Maimonides' later years, he moved strongly toward rationalism. Truth demanded that Aristotle be satisfied, as well as Moses. In Steinberg's spiritual pilgrimage, he returned in his last years to traditional sources of inspiration. He began to wear the traditional phylacteries in morning prayer.

A year after his death, a tombstone was erected over his grave. It was simple: the only words were: RABBI MILTON STEINBERG and the years of his birth and death. Below, were inscribed three words:

FAITH   AND   REASON.

Over the years since 1951, circumstances brought me to the cemetery, and I passed the memorial stone regularly. Two bushes had been planted, one on each corner of the plot. Evidently, the two bushes had flourished, as shrubbery will, with differing degrees of success. One year, I noticed that the word, FAITH, had virtually been covered by the left bush. Only MILTON STEINBERG and REASON were visible. Then, either Nature or a gardener intervened, and FAITH emerged, with REASON obliterated. Years later, the first four letters of FAITH were covered, and all of REASON had disappeared. All that remained were four letters: H. . . . AND. Milton's young admirer, Judy, would probably have beheld a divine Hand hovering over her rabbi.

On my last visits to the Westchester cemetery, Nature and the gardener seemed finally to have resolved their differences, and the situation was stabilized. REASON had all but vanished. Only FAITH remained.

*   *   *

I have spent a half-century grappling with the basic problems of religion, indeed, trying to catch a glimpse of its true essence. When I began to worry that the tentativeness of my convictions implied a kind of emotional or intellectual instability on my part, I was reassured when I heard my guide and mentor, Mordecai M. Kaplan, (who enjoys good physical health and clarity of mind in his mid-nineties) tell me, only a dozen years ago, that he is still searching for the answers. And he has been probing for truths for over seven decades.

I suggested to Doctor Kaplan that a verse in the Psalms, incorporated in our liturgy, offered a clue to our problem. "Light dawns for the *righteous*—and gladness for the *upright in heart.*" The English translation misses a thought expressed in the original Hebrew text. The first line of the verse, referring to "the righteous", is singular. The second line, referring to "the upright in heart", is plural. Possibly, the author of the Psalms was telling us that "light"—the ultimate truth—is reserved for no more than one righteous one in a generation. For the rest of us fallible human beings, the most we can aspire to is a bit of "gladness of heart" that comes in the wake of our quest.

When I was fourteen, I was certain that I had found the truth. The final word was the Revelation out of Sinai. Tradition was inflexible, unyielding. I embraced Orthodoxy with an enthusiasm which disconcerted my parents. My father, David, was a Hebrew scholar, a lover of Zion, but not well disposed toward the rigidities of Orthodoxy. He had fled from Russia, not to escape the wrath of the Czars, but to find refuge from the narrow pieties of the Hasidim in his native town.

Within five years, my studies of anthropology, sociology and comparative religions had made inroads on my orthodoxy. But in the meantime I had succeeded in converting my parents to traditional observances. My mother abandoned her Saturday morning shopping; my father began to attend Orthodox services with some regularity. In the sunset of their lives, they were utterly at a loss to understand how their son, the erstwhile evangelist of the family, had fallen on erring ways to embrace liberalism.

Through the years, I shared my father's distaste for the Hasidic movement. In Toronto, we could not com-

prehend modern, intelligent Jews following the Rebbe
with a blind faith, because he was one of the many descendants of the original Master of the Good Name, the
founder of an 18th century movement, based on faith
rather than intellect.

At times, we found their unworldliness amusing. The
Stretiner Rebbe, our local Hasidic leader, one of the
scions of the Hasidic dynasty, preached a sermon on
divine judgment, dramatizing his belief that all of us
would some day stand before the heavenly Throne of
Judgment.

"What happens," he asked, "when a trial takes place
here in our city? First, the litigants present their cases to
the Toronto Municipal Court. When one side loses, he
may appeal to the Supreme Court of Ontario; later, he
may take his case to the Supreme Court of Canada, in
Ottawa. When all else fails, he may appeal to the Privy
Council in *London*. Finally, if he loses in London, there
is one last court of appeal, the Supreme Court in *Washington*. But, my dear people, there is one Court still
higher: the Heavenly Tribunal before which all must
stand in judgment!"

In the Old World, we would have been called, *misnag-
dim*, opponents of the Hasidim, who lacked faith in the
miraculous powers of the Rebbes. One favorite tale of
the Opponents was of a great Rebbe who came to a
synagogue in Lithuania, the very hotbed of opposition!
In the middle of a sermon, he was heckled by a sceptic.
Angrily, the Rebbe ordained that the walls of the synagogue should cave in and destroy the mockers. As the
miracle was about to take place, one of his disciples
pleaded:

"How can you do this, Rebbe? The innocent will
suffer with the guilty. Innocent mothers and children!

The Rebbe, moved to compassion, ordained that a sec-

ond miracle should occur. Let the four walls remain
unmoved. Lo and behold, the wonder-working Rebbe
succeeded: two miracles followed in quick succession,
one upon the other!

These were my memories when I recently travelled to
the headquarters of the world-renowned Hasidic leader,
Rabbi Menachem Mendel Schneerson, known as the
Lubavitcher Rebbe. Unquestionably, the rabbi has the
largest Jewish congregation in the world, numbering
well over one hundred thousand followers in every continent. The nerve-center of the movement is in Brooklyn.

I was prepared for some of the experiences of that
night. It was night, rather than evening, because the
rabbi's schedule of appointments extends from ten in the
evening until five in the morning. He sleeps two hours
a night, and devotes the rest of his waking moments to
prayer and study. We waited till near midnight in his
outer office where an active telephone switchboard took
calls from Buenos Aires, Paris and Jerusalem. The out-
posts of his movement reach to virtually every community in the world. The Rebbe's disciples represent all
walks of life: a scientist in Oxford, a captain of industry
in Los Angeles, college students, peddlers, and thousands of young men, many of them married, who devote
all their time to study.

I remembered Carlyle's definition, "Faith is loyalty to
some inspired teacher, some spiritual hero." Those who
were waiting in the halls outside his office—there must
have been a hundred despite the early hours of the morning—regarded the seventy-year-old Rebbe as their
spiritual hero. His background is most unusual for a
miracle-working rabbi. The Rebbe was trained as an
engineer in the Sorbonne, Paris; his wife was a student
of architecture. But dynastic demands—leadership is

transmitted from father to son, or to the closest kin—summoned him to assume responsibility as head of the movement.

One suppliant was there to seek advice on a proposed marriage for his son. No disciple would consider entering into a marriage arrangement without consultation with and approval of the Rebbe. Another was considering the soundness of a business offer in Montreal. A third hoped that the rabbi's blessing would put an end to her childlessness.

What does a saint look like when you are face to face with him? How does he act? Does he "hold court?"—remain aloof, patronizing, condescending? How is he garbed?

Rabbi Schneerson's private office was remarkably unpretentious, the furniture simple and threadbare. The Rebbe was less than average in height, and had a gray-black beard. He was clad in the traditional garb, a long silk coat, and his head covering was not the expected skull-cap—Hasidim wear hats at all times—but a large-brimmed black fedora. My companion, who had visited the Rebbe annually for the past twenty years, later told me that the fedora was the very same one that the rabbi had worn in the 1950's.

The Rebbe was at home in ten languages, and spoke in English, mixed with a few Hebrew and Yiddish quotations. His manner was straight-forward, without a trace of imperiousness. He shared with us his concern for the spiritual nurture of children. They needed more schools, and they needed them now. "Childhood can't wait," he lamented.

Near the end of an hour-long interview, he asked if we knew any New York City officials. We might be helpful in solving a problem. High-rise apartments were being erected in the Brownsville section of Brooklyn, for the use of low-income families. Many of his followers had applied for apartments; they met all the requirements. Would we be good enough to ask the Housing officials for one favor: grant his people priority in assignment of the first three floors? Jewish law forbade them to use elevators on Sabbaths and holydays. It seemed a reasonable request.

"I would ask you, when you speak to the authorities, don't formulate the request on behalf of *Hasidic* Jews, *observant* Jews, *Orthodox* Jews—just Jews."

One of our group raised an eyebrow. After all, there were some of our people who did use elevators on the Sabbath.

The Rebbe studied our faces for a moment. His eyes were the color of the sky on a clear, bright day. They seemed to be contemplating us and, at the same time, to be communing with some power above and beyond us.

"Just say, Jews. You know, what a Jew does *this* Sabbath is no guarantee what he will do *next* Sabbath."

The Rebbe didn't seem to be talking about observant Jews, or his own Hasidic followers, or any Jews. He was reflecting a deeply felt and oft-articulated belief of his that human beings can be changed. All it took was faith.

As I left his study, I could hear my father wondering how I had permitted myself to become enmeshed in the Rebbe's spell. In the hall-way, some of the after-midnight crowd, most of whom had no particular business with the Rebbe, touched the hems of our raincoats as we were putting them on. "Were you actually in the presence of the sainted one? What morsels of wisdom fell from his lips?"

My raincoat had taken on a contagious sanctity, and I felt myself welcoming the opportunity of shedding the Rebbe's holiness in a vicarious way. I even quoted one or two improvised aphorisms we had heard. My father's son.

Some time ago, on one of my trans-Atlantic voyages, I attended a Sabbath shipboard service. I sat next to a Hasid, a disciple of the Rebbe. Following worship, as we walked out together, we exchanged thoughts about the Torah portion—the lesson from Scriptures—which we had just heard. My companion was dressed in the special silk raiment worn by Hasidim on the Sabbath.

He seemed delighted with our common realm of discourse although he knew that I was a liberal rabbi. As we parted at the door of my cabin, he shook my hand—and my composure, too—with a final word: "Who knows—perhaps, in the sight of God, you are as pleasing to Him as I am!"

Faith and Reason. He had one answer. I, another. Who knows if in God's sight . . . ?

Psychic Phenomena

When is coincidence more than coincidence?

That was the question which my university class in Philosophy of Religion grappled with in our 8 A.M. session. For an entire hour, the students argued about the validity of claims made by several of the class members that psychic phenomena were a reality. We examined some of the experimental work done by Professor Rhine at Duke University involving extra-sensory perception. A few reported nocturnal dreams that had come true. One girl described a vivid premonition of disaster before a tragic loss in the family. And I related experiences which I had had that seemed to validate the thesis that mind and matter are not too far apart.

On more than one occasion, there had flashed into my mind a very clear image of a person whom I had not seen for many years. I was walking on 42nd Street in New York when, for no reason I could explain, I conjured up an image of a Canadian friend whom I hadn't met in a dozen years. I turned the corner on Fifth Avenue, and, two blocks away, I bumped into him! Had he been sending out waves?

The 8:50 bell rang, and the students moved out, still arguing their respective claims. One of them pressed the point that "It was only coincidence." Her friend countered with the conviction that it was more than coincidence.

The 9 A.M. Ancient Religions students began to arrive, and one of them stopped at my desk to ask a question.

"Prof. Kertzer, on Monday, we discussed the story of the battle of Jericho, and you told about archeologist Garstang who had dug up proof that an earthquake had caused the walls to tumble down. I wonder if Garstang is still alive."

Her question caught me off-guard. I had forgotton the date of the Garstang excavations: it was some time earlier in the century. I should have pleaded ignorance, but I confidently answered,

"He must be dead by now." Young teachers, like their contemporaries, find it hard to imagine living beyond the biblical three score years and ten.

As we spoke, my secretary entered the lecture hall and informed me that a colleague of mine wanted me on the phone. It was some sort of emergency. I glanced at my watch: there were two minutes left before the 9 o'clock class.

"Kertzer, this is Trowbridge. Sorry to take you away from class, but something just came up. Are you free for dinner tonight?"

My schedule was clear. "I'd like you to join us at the Jefferson Hotel. We have a house guest who just arrived from Turkey. You may know him: Prof. John Garstang."

A Seat in Heaven

The historic cities of the world are generally associated with a single theme: Florence with art; Vienna with music; Istanbul and Bangkok with Oriental faiths and religious architecture. One small city in Israel, Safed, has an unusual historic product, mysticism. For hundreds of years its raison d'etre was a cabalistic search for religious truth. Scholars converged on the town in the 12th and 14th centuries with only one purpose in mind: to search for God through mystical communion.

How much of the mysticism was fed by the precariousness of life, it is hard to estimate. Like their Chilean and Peruvian counterparts, the people of Safed lived constantly on cliff's edge. In 1742, the town was devastated by plague, and seventeen years later an earthquake wiped out the last traces of the community. Undaunted, a new group of truth-seekers, this time from Lithuania and the Ukraine, left their academies of classic study to rebuild the mystic capital. It was the magic year of 1776! And in 1837, a new earthquake toppled all the academies and many of the synagogues, burying most of the cabalists in graves fashioned by nature and, for a decade or more, untouched by human hands.

Across from my hotel room on the main street of modern Safed, I had purchased a few books at a small shop.

I noticed the name on the window: Luria.

An intriguing name. The year was 1969 and I recalled from my history books that back in 1569 the founder of modern Cabala, Rabbi Isaac Luria, had moved from his native Jerusalem to found a center of mysticism not more than a few blocks from where we were standing. (You could walk there by descending a few hundred steps.)

"Are you any relation to *the* Isaac Luria?" I asked.

He nodded in the affirmative as he kept wrapping the package.

"I understand that the Luria dynasty traced its ancestry back to King David and King Solomon."

"Of course, all we Lurias are of the House of David."

He picked up a string and continued his labors.

"I suppose you know that, comes the Messiah, the Day of Final Resurrection, all Jews will be gathered to Jerusalem. The Talmud tells us that there'll be room for everybody."

By now the package was neatly tied. As he handed it to me, he continued in a matter-of-fact way, "You probably know that there will be only enough seats in Jerusalem for those of us of the House of David. The rest of you Jews will have to stand—forever. Thanks for your purchase. Sholom. Sholom."

On the following Sabbath my wife and I were on the lower level of the city. Even though we were well below the 3,000 foot top of Safed, we could still look out at the panorama of Upper Galilee. We began the steep ascent on the mountain slope and we estimated that there were about three to four hundred steps to negotiate in the warm July sun. About a third of the way up, we stopped to catch our breath. Our destination was a historic synagogue, one of the centers of ancient mysticism, where a class in Bible study was being held for women students.

A tiny old lady, very ancient, caught up to us at the landing. She, too, was on her way to the Bible session. We asked her age.

"I'm ninety-nine years old, a great-great-grandmother. I've been a midwife all my life. Many of 'my babies' are now great-grandmothers. Do you know that when you're a great-grandmother, you are automatically guaranteed a seat in Heaven?"

We continued our upward climb, a bit envious of the nonagenarian's agility. She had been scaling these steps for almost a century.

"Yes, we're guaranteed a seat in Heaven. But the trouble is, by the time you're a great-grandmother, you are too old to sin!"

What Can You Believe In?

The call came just before midnight on Saturday.

"Bernie has been in an automobile accident. He's in very bad shape." The hospital was only a mile from my home.

"Should I come right over? Is he in intensive care?"

"No, of course not. Tomorrow morning is all right."

At eight on Sunday morning, I stood at the door of his hospital room. A medium-sized band-aid was plastered on Bernie's forehead. No other visible injuries. But it was obvious from Bernie's clouded eyes that he had not slept that night. He breathed heavily.

"Bernie, what happened? Is your chest all right?" Apparently it was.

"Rabbi, it's a long story. Sarah Jane and I were on our way to a New York theater, but we never made it."

"Were you in your Rolls-Royce?"

"That's it, rabbi, the Rolls Royce." He blinked back some tears.

"Since I was a small boy on Allen Street, I dreamed of owning a Rolls Royce. We had no money. I helped to support my parents, even in high school. I worked hard on Seventh Avenue till today I have over six hundred workers in my plant. Years ago, I had to go to England on business. The London people sent a limousine and a chauffeur to meet me at the airport. A Rolls Royce! I sat back, and I said to myself, 'this is for me. Some day, I'll own a Rolls-Royce. A regular *Rock of Gibraltar!* A solid rock!'

"Last night, we were going down Second Avenue, in the 60's, and I stopped for a traffic light. One car was waiting in front of me, a compact. All of a sudden, a guy comes from around the corner, and bang! He pushed me into the other car. You won't believe this, rabbi. The compact car in front, the compact car in back—hardly a scratch. My Rolls-Royce . . ." He wiped the perspiration off his brow. "My Rolls-Royce . . . was smashed in. Front and back."

Clumsily, I expressed the thought that, at least he was all in one piece.

"What do you mean, rabbi? One piece? What's the use of living? If you can't trust a Rolls-Royce, *what can you believe in?* Everything I ever dreamed about, everything I believed in—it's gone! A Rock of Gibraltar—it's gone!"

Under the Sidewalks of New York

New Yorkers are aware that many of the stereotypes about them bear little resemblance to fact. The out-of-towner (I admit that New Yorkers do divide the world into New York and out of town) visualizes the typical metropolitan rider, on commuter train or subway, as a person buried in his *News* or *Times*, encasing himself in a shell of remoteness and indifference, zealously protecting his privacy.

My experience, both as a commuter on the Long Island Railroad and on all the branches of the City's subways, has often been the opposite.

Riding on the South Shore Line of the Long Island Railroad every weekday, for a dozen years, provided me with a liberal education in Americana. On that particular line, the commuter trains begin, before dawn, from the eastern tip of the island. The Protestants climb aboard first, having moved to "exurbia" to escape the rest of us; the Jews join them at the midway suburban stations; finally, the Catholics board at the City's outer rim—and the ecumenical trainload is greeted at Penn Station by the blacks and the Puerto Ricans.

There is a kind of gentlemen's agreement that guarantees a silent treatment to Long Island passengers while they read their newspapers or do their office homework.

One notable exception to that rule are the Board members of Jewish congregations from Babylon to Valley Stream. I did not have to attend their meetings to obtain complete verbal minutes of their deliberations.

On many occasions, I suffered vicariously through problems of budget balancing. "Does the Cantor really need a raise? I think we've gone the limit with our rabbi? Who tells them to have a baby every year?"

Even the most determined efforts not to eavesdrop are useless when the commuter debate centers on a conflict about the rabbi's tenure. The rule, handed down by the national organization, presents a dilemma. Elect the rabbi for his tenth year, and he's yours for life.

"His sermons aren't what they used to be." "A new rabbi will cost us less." "My Sally saw the rabbi's wife in Long Beach, wearing a bikini."

The prize comment came from the lips of a visiting North Shore Temple officer.

"The other night, I phoned the rabbi and asked him to come to Aqueduct with me on Wednesday. I told him that my partner, Kelly, took his priest to the track to pick out the horses, half for the Church and half for Kelly. You won't believe this. The rabbi turned me down! And here we are in the midst of a big building campaign."

I grant that the subway rider, within New York's five boroughs, is considerably more introverted than his Long Island counterpart. Within a few months after I moved to New York, I was taught the wisdom of minding one's own business.

On a quiet Sunday afternoon, I was on a local Lexington Avenue subway train as it came to the Grand Central stop. Near the door, three passengers gathered around their suitcases, picked them up, and hurried out. One of their bags was left behind. Fortunately, the subway door remained open for over a minute. During those frenzied seconds, a number of us, obviously tourists, argued about the best Good Samaritan plan. A young man held the door open and shouted to the departing passengers on their way up the stairs. They were well out of hearing range.

I had a bolder idea. Why not shove the luggage out to the platform? The forgetful passengers would probably notice their loss when they checked their baggage and might return to the subway platform in the hope that some ingenious person would have done just what I was proposing. The *ad hoc* committee was about to implement my plan when the door slammed shut.

The train moved out of the station through the tunnel. At the next stop, 33rd Street, a man, at the other end of the car, who had apparently been so absorbed in his newspaper that he had not shared our agony, calmly walked up to claim his suitcase, and, without a word, picked it up and stepped off the train!

Passengers, on the local subway trains, may be of a different breed than regular express riders. On an Independent line train, which had its origin in the Bronx, a middle-aged man, sitting across the aisle, raised his voice above the screech of the wheels:

"You look like a lawyer."

"No, I'm not a lawyer," I called back.

"But you *look* like a lawyer."

I kept answering him that I was not an attorney, but he was unconvinced.

"I got a big problem. . . . My wife is going to have a baby."

"Mazol tov." I assumed that the Bronx passenger would understand my Jewish felicitations.

"What mazol tov? I'm not the father of the baby. That's my problem!

The train had stopped at 96th Street, and I was able to

lower my voice. "The next stop is mine. Sorry, I have to get off."

"Please, mister, how about staying on one more stop, to 72nd Street. You gotta help."

I rose from my seat. I volunteered the name of a Bronx rabbi. From the 86th Street platform, I called through the train window.

"Look up his number in the Bronx phone-book. He's right on Grand Concourse."

An express train ride, from the outer reaches of Queens to the heart of Manhattan, can permit a counselling session. A young lady, at my side, struck up a conversation. (Does my profession show on my face or is it simply that familiarity is bred by long train travel?) Her accent was small town, Southern.

She lived in a small Louisiana town, and was returning to her soldier husband stationed in Connecticut.

"Ah've been visiting with mah kinfolk, his and mahn."

From Kew Gardens to 59th Street, she unfolded her life-story. Her first meeting her husband; the vigorous opposition of both sets of parents; and their persistent interference during the two years of their marriage. She had long straight flaxen hair and a pretty freckled face.

"This visit was the worst of all. Jim's parents were *so* mean. Ever since we've been married they keep telling me not to have a baby!"

I muttered a few words of commiseration.

"Jim and Ah would *love* to have a baby. But Jim's folks won't. . . ."

As I stood up to leave the train, I looked at her face, and a flash of inspiration occurred to me.

"You say you've been married two years. That's hard to believe. How old are you?"

She waved good bye. "Oh, Ahm fifteen."

Original Paintings

My friend, Norman Kraft, had acquired a priceless collection of art during his long lifetime. As we met at lunch, in his Club, he showed me a booklet, issued by the Los Angeles Museum of Art, to publicize a showing of his rare collection, on loan.

Among his prized possessions, were the works of Van Gogh, Renoir, Matisse, Degas and Modigliani.

That day, my wife and I were celebrating our twenty-fifth wedding anniversary; Norman and his wife had just marked their golden anniversary. In jest, I suggested that he might offer us one of his paintings on our fiftieth wedding anniversary.

"Why wait for your golden one? I'll send you one of my paintings for your silver."

A week later, the package came. In an exquisite frame, was an original Kraft painting, done by my friend Norman.

His artistic painting of his brother Jules, on a bridge in Provincetown, remained in our closet for a number of years, but it was hung on our living-room wall every time Norman visited our home.

Tell It to the Chaplain

I wondered how the two of them had been able to communicate with each other. At least, to get acquainted to the point of being engaged to be married. The sergeant, sitting in my chaplain's office in Dijon, France, came from a farm in Oklahoma. She spoke only French. It wasn't easy for me to decipher his backwoods drawl. With her limited English vocabulary, how were they able to develop a relationship that brought them to me with wedding plans?

Overseas chaplains had been alerted to the problems of hasty army marriages, stimulated by soldier loneliness and the calculated desire of French (or Italian or Belgian) girls to gain entrance into the United States. One method to discourage them was to slow down the process of granting permission, in the hope that the soldier might be shipped out. That was the nub of the problem before me.

The slowing-down procedure consisted of piling up military paper-work: the application for permission to marry had to be approved by the company commander, then channelled upward through battalion, regimental, division, and, finally, Base Section commands; then returned through the same army labyrinth in reverse—a process that consumed about three months.

I spoke to Thérèse, an attractive French girl, in her native language. Their papers were stalled somewhere, and they suspected the source of the delay. The Oklahoman complained:

"I know who's holding up permission. My application went all the way up to your headquarters. We got approval from your office. But, on its way back, it got stuck in battalion. Major T. won't sign, because he's living with Thérèse, and he won't give her up!"

Was I following his hill-country English? I watched Thérèse's face. Did she understand what he was saying?

"C'est vrai? Mademoiselle, avec M. le Commandant?" (Is that true? You and the major . . . ?")

Thérèse replied demurely:

"Oui, mon capitaine, oui. Mais, apres le mariage, fini!" (Yes, captain, but after the marriage—finished!")

* * *

The suggestion, "Go tell it to the chaplain." when it came from a soldier's commanding officer or his sergeant, generally meant: "Only God can help you. He has an office down the road." Barracks' language for the same advice was more earthy. In mock sympathy, a soldier was told to have his chaplain punch his T.S. (explanation deleted) card.

Many of the G.I. problems were beyond remedy. "My wife had a baby last week, and I haven't been in the States for over a year."

At Fort Dix, where I served in the Reception Center, a New York soldier came in to complain. His mother was not receiving his allotment check.

"Why worry about that now? You've only been in the army a couple of days." (The average stay at the Reception Center was less than six days.) "How long have you been here?"

"I got here last January." (It was now mid-June.)

Was he part of the permanent staff? He shook his head.

"Let's start from the beginning. You were inducted at Grand Central Palace?"

"What's 'inducted'? What do you mean, Grand Central Palace?"

"You go to the Induction Center, raise your right hand, and you're sworn into the army."

Nothing like that had happened to him. How did he get to Fort Dix?

"It's a long story, chaplain. Last New Year's Eve, I was at a farewell party for one of my buddies who was going into the army. We had some drinks, a lot of drinks, and we all went down to Penn Station to see him off. That was some crowd! I couldn't move. Everyone kept pushing and shoving. I found myself on a train, and I must have fallen asleep. Maybe four in the morning, the train stops, and I get off with the rest of the fellows. A guy yells, 'Fall in line, two rows.' I start walking away, and some other guy yells, 'Back in line, you s.o.b., where do you think you're going?' "Home," I says, and, he says, 'that's what you think.' I argued, 'I don't belong here.' 'That's what they all say.'

"They gave me a physical, and put me in the Station Hospital for syphilis. I was there for a month, with other things as well. On the first of the month, all I get is five dollars pay. No allotment."

I picked up the phone and called the master-sergeant at Company E.

"Do you have anyone on morning report named J . . . ?"

He was on morning report, one overload, but his records were at the Hospital. The hospital sergeant informed me that the man's records were at company headquarters.

"Do you have a serial number? How about dog-tags?"

He had both. A mystified classification clerk, months

back, had improvised a number and had issued the dog-
tags.

What had he been doing all these past months? Well,
he had taken off for home every week-end, even though
new inductees were restricted to the Post. I found out
later that his Draft Board began looking for him in April,
and officially had declared him a draft dodger.

What was his status now? I called Post headquarters,
and consulted the Judge Advocate's office.

"Had he ever signed a payroll?" I mentioned the Station Hospital episode of the five dollar pay-check.

"Then he's in the army."

If he hadn't sought out the chaplain about his mother's
allotment check, he might have remained undisturbed at
the 1229th Reception Center until after V-J Day, and
would probably have received top priority before the
post-war Amnesty Board.

*   *   *

One week, I was sure that I had detected anti-semitism
in the Army. Several draftees reported to me, on succes-
sive days, that they had been asked by the Classification
clerk if they were Zionists. What business was it of the
army's to inquire whether a Jewish inductee had any
interest in the restoration of Palestine as a Jewish home-
land?

The complainants had a number of things in common.
They had all attended the City College of New York;
they were Jewish; and were readers of either *The Nation*,
The New Republic, or *PM*, a New York liberal daily published by Marshall Field. I had heard rumors that the
Classification Office, which had, apparently, never been
given a score-card indicating who was on our team in the
War, and, who placed the initials, S.D., (suspected dis-
loyalty) on the top right-hand corner of a soldier's 201-
file.

I decided against a frontal attack. Frequently, I played

ping-pong with one of the Classification officers. He would solve the mystery about the Zionist question.

At the officer's club, as we batted the ball back and forth, I casually asked:

"Schmo, (his real name was much more unbelievable than "Schmo") what's this about Zionists in your interviews?"

He put down his ping-pong paddle. "Isn't that a great idea?"

The officer, who had spent his entire life in a Southern village which had no Jews, had made a marvellous discovery.

"You know, chaplain, we ask a lot of questions about the G.I.'s background. One day, I put it bluntly to a City College fellow, "Are you a Communist?"

" 'No,' he answered, 'I'm a Zionist.' "

"What in the heck is a Zionist? Never heard that word before.

"The G.I. spent about half an hour explaining to me that a Jew can't be a Communist and a Zionist at the same time. The Communists hate the Zionists. Isn't that great? I told my clerks that, when they interview one of those City College folks, just to ask them if they are Zionists. Saves a lot of time."

* * *

A chaplain's flock on our overseas assignment often included the native population. In Marseille, a local resident came to our office with a pained anxious look on his face.

"Do you happen to know Captain L.? Perhaps you have some influence over him?"

I had met the Port Battalion officer.

"Rabbi, I appreciate his visits. I haven't been working for over a year. The captain brings us food packages and toys for the children. He once brought a parachute, so my wife would make some silk dresses for herself. But, he comes *too often.*"

The shy little man lowered his voice as he came to the heart of his problem. "Every time the captain visits my wife, she makes me spend the evening in the basement. Once a week, I don't mind. But four times a week! Would you please tell the captain? . . . ?"

* * *

On the Anzio beachhead, one of our chaplains was delighted at every opportunity to baptize one of the men in our Division. We had heard stories about his Pacific counterpart, a chaplain in far-off Guadalcanal. They called him, "Be-dipped-or-be-damned Jones."

Captain K. was importuned by a news photographer, covering the beachhead, to permit pictures to be taken of a baptism. Sammie, the photographer, was not satisfied with one shot, and persuaded both chaplain and soldier to repeat the ritual a second time. The second shot, he explained, was to be taken from the water, with Anzio as a perfect background. Still, Sammie was not satisfied. He wanted a shot at another angle, and the good-natured chaplain agreed to a third baptism of the soldier.

For quite a long time afterward, Captain K. avoided our Officers' Mess during the busy hours. His fellow-officers would bait him:

"What kind of a Baptist are you? You dipped your soldier once for God—and twice for Sammie Goldstein!"

* * *

"Who takes care of your problems, chaplain?"

I heard that question often. I found the answer on the last day of military service.

After two tours of duty in the European Theater, I returned to Fort Dix, New Jersey, this time under the jurisdiction of its Separation Center. My father had died a few months before, and my mother had recently suffered a heart attack in her Toronto, Canada, home. I couldn't wait to be at her side. Routine separation procedures lasted three days, and I climbed the walls during the painful wait.

On the third day, several hundred army officers were ushered into the Fort Dix auditorium. The speaker was a captain.

"Gentlemen, I know how eager you all are to get home, but we have just one final step before separation. As your name is called, please go into one of the cubicles outside the hall. The men, who are sitting on either side of me here on the stage, will spend about fifteen minutes with each of you. We want to talk a bit about the problems of civilian life. Your name will be called in alphabetical order. The last man ought to be out in five hours."

My heart fell. The letter "K" would not be reached for over two hours, too late for the last daily train to Toronto. Plane reservations were out of the question.

The officer ended with a word of farewell, and then added:

"Will Captain Kertzer please come forward."

Startled, I assumed that he had a message of bad news from Toronto. The captain motioned me to follow him into one of the cubicles.

"I see you don't recognize me in uniform. You may not recall this, but, when I was working on my doctorate in psychology at the University of Iowa, my wife Susan went to the hospital to have our first baby. We didn't know a soul in town, since we had arrived only recently. There wasn't enough money for my folks to come West. It was a terrifyingly lonely experience for both of us. Your wife was Susan's only visitor. She came every day; even brought our baby a layette—our first baby gift. We'll never forget both of you. . . . Good afternoon, and good luck."

I just made the train.

"The Rabbi Doesn't Know the Bible!"

Religious leaders, since time immemorial, have been rather ambivalent about the question of liquid spirits. In my own tradition, Judaism, we have leaned quite heavily on the biblical counsel, "wine rejoiceth the heart of man." Alcohol, in immoderate measure, is, of course, taboo. And, happily, alcoholism is rather rare in Jewish life. But there are some occasions in Jewish religious observance when wine is required—at circumcisions, at weddings, on Sabbaths and festivals. Though I happen to limit myself to "the fruit of the vine," I must admit that my more observant brethren embrace stronger beverages as an integral part of their diet. Hasidim, particularly, see no conflict between their rigid pieties and a rather free use of brandy and whiskey.

Does the dictionary coincidence of the term, spirits, and the word, spiritual, possibly suggest that there are solid connections between the two? Anthropologists have long noted the relationship in more primitive forms of religion. But sometimes I wonder if modern man has not found a bio-chemical connection.

At midnight, I received a long distance telephone message that an unnamed person was trying to reach me. Call Operator 26 in Fort Smith, Arkansas. I could not recall knowing anyone in western Arkansas. I returned the call, and was connected with a hotel cocktail lounge

in Fort Smith. One of my neighbors, a travelling sales-
man, had been imbibing with some business associates,
and their late-hour discussion had kindled a heated theological debate. He placed a call to me, and invited me to
settle the dispute.

Aboard a small ship in the Mediterranean, I walked up
to the bar and ordered a glass of lemonade. The radio
officer of the ship recognized me. It was evident that he
had been glued to his bar seat for several hours.

"Hey, fellas, here's a rabbi who doesn't know his Bible!"

I was taken aback by this challenge to my biblical
credentials, and asked him what he meant. (The Talmud
warns "Don't mix with drunks!")

"That water you're drinking. Where in all the Bible
does it mention that water is used for drinking?"

"How about Rebecca going to the well?"

"Oh, that was to take care of her camels."

"What about Moses beating the rock and turning it
into water?"

"That was for washing his hands."

I cited a few more passages from Holy Scriptures that
pointedly referred to drinking water, and I felt confident
that I had won over the saloon jury by my documented
arguments. The cornered officer fell back on a new theological stratagem.

"You'll admit, rabbi, that our good Lord never created
anything in vain. For everything on earth there is a
purpose. If God Almighty hadn't wanted us to drink
scotch, He wouldn't have invented it!"

I lost the jury.

Transition

It was quite a wrench for six-year old Deirdre. Three months ago, her mother had embraced the Jewish faith. I officiated at the solemn conversion rites in the presence of the proselyte's mother, Deirdre's grandmother, who attended Catholic Mass seven days a week, and several of her aunts and uncles who took communion regularly.

Though Deidre's step-father, Stanley, had brought her to Temple on occasion, her confusion could not have entirely evaporated that week when she attended her first grade class at Our Lady of Sorrows School in Westchester the first two days, and, allowing only one day for the transition, was transferred to a Long Island Synagogue School that Thursday.

Early in January, Deirdre and her mother came to visit me.

"How do you like your new school?" I asked her.

The youngster's bright-blue eyes sparkled.

"I love it. Sister Moskowitz told us all about Chanukah!"

If You Can't Fight Them, Join Them

Religious traditions and modern technology are engaged in a constant tug-of-war. Some practices that had remained unchanged for thousands of years, under the threat of every conceivable persecution—the burning-stake, pogroms, inquisitions, gas chambers—face the logistics of a technological society which have played havoc with age-old rituals. A Jewish girl, in a college dormitory, wants to kindle Sabbath candles in her room. Fire regulations forbid it. An Eternal Light in a synagogue must never be extinguished. But, oil lamps are too cumbersome, and a dim electric bulb is substituted. Even then, the Temple receives a call: "Because of the energy crisis, would you mind turning off your Eternal (sic) Light, except during worship?"

The observant Jew has resourcefully discovered ways of utilizing modern technology for the service of God. Forbidden to turn on a light switch on the Sabbath, or to turn it off, Orthodox Jews attach a timing device, or some type of mechanism, that does the labor. One of the Ten Commandments forbids "any manner of work, neither thou . . . nor thy manservant, nor thy maidservant." The Bible does not mention photo-electric cells.

For a time, elevators created a crisis for Sabbath-observers. Dr. Solomon Schechter, one of the first presidents of the Jewish Theological Seminary, at the turn of the century, lived on the ninth floor of his apartment building. His students reported that, when they joined him for Sabbath dinner, he pointed to the stairs—"you boys walk"—and he took the elevator. The Sabbath ban was horizontal, not vertical.

Today's observant Jews will ride in an elevator on the Sabbath only on condition that they do not activate it by pressing a button. In a Jewish Home for the Aged, that I visited, I saw a sign: "This elevator stops at every floor on the Sabbath and holydays." The other one did not.

A few years ago, a new Orthodox synagogue was established in the fashionable part of New York's Fifth Avenue district. The *New York Times* reported a remarkable engineering feat in connection with the new building. The synagogue elevator was designed to carry the male worshippers one flight up, to *their* level, and female worshippers, to the next level. The whole procedure was automatic, without the use of a button.

I clipped the story, and carried it with me to an Army Signal Corps base where I was scheduled to deliver a lecture. At a dinner with a few senior officers, all electronic experts, I showed the *Times* story, and asked how they would program an elevator to make a distinction between the sexes. We all took the Times story seriously. One colonel speculated that, by placing a light beam at a certain spot, a skirt would break the circuit, and pants would not. (He did not have to allow for either mini-skirts or slacks: this was an Orthodox house of worship.) Another colonel thought that a light beam, at the five-foot four level, would be more effective. As a general rule, men are over that height; women are not. I later learned that the newspaper story was inaccurate: the elevator stopped automatically at all floors.

What happens to other historic faiths which face the

same problems of technological assault? A Buddhist editor, whom I visited in Tokyo, told me that he had been
on a flight from Tokyo to Nepal, to attend a World
Buddhist Conference. He was a Mahayana (loosely, liberal) Buddhist, dressed in Western style. At the Bangkok
airport, a number of saffron-robed monks came on
board. He spoke, across the aisle, to them:

"Aren't you violating one of your most sacred vows?
Theravada monks swear a solemn oath not to travel
aboard a vessel which carried women passengers."

The Thai monks were not at a loss for an answer.

"That ancient vow covers only land and sea vessels. It
does not apply to sky travel!"

"But there is another vow you are breaking. Your vow
of poverty forbids you to carry money."

"That's no problem. We carry no money—only tra-
vellers' checks."

* * *

Moses wrote a code of laws for all generations, and all
seasons. Could he have foreseen a situation when 20th
century travel would provide stumbling blocks for the
faithful? At least two unprecedented problems were
placed before the Law Committee of the Jewish Welfare
Board Chaplain's Commission:

1) During World War II, a stream of military tran-
sports moved across the Pacific. How do you observe the
Sabbath when your New-Guinea bound ship crosses the
International Dateline just as the sun is setting on Friday
evening? The Sabbath literally disappears.

2) You are required to usher in the Sabbath at sunset.
How do you do that at Kiska, Alaska, when there is no
sunset for months?

* * *

Of course, both churches and synagogue have taken
advantage of the new tools of modern technology, such

as creative use of multa-media material in teaching. But no religionist can compare in ingenuity with the late evangelist, Aimee Semple McPherson, whose great instinct for drama excited a whole generation. In the vast California auditorium, which she built for her Four Square Gospel, she ordered a long ramp to be erected, leading up to the speaker's rostrum. As the choir sang the opening hymn, a motor-cycle roared up the runway, its motor wide-open. The motorcycle screeched to a swerving halt at the rostrum, and the helmeted revivalist leaped off, shouting: "We are all riding straight to Hell!"

* * *

Even those who are not bound by the strict demands of ancient Law have occasion to grapple with modern technology.

On the first Sunday of October, 1947, I was returning from a graveside service in the outer reaches of Brooklyn. It was a long ride back to Manhattan. Seated in the limousine were the mourners, including a famous songwriter. He had just lost his older brother. As we rode down Ocean Parkway, there was an air of excitement everywhere. This was the Day of Judgment for the embattled Brooklyn Dodgers; the sixth game of the World Series; their last chance to remain in the Series. We could hear the blare of radio announcers each time a taxi passed us. The mourning brother solicited my opinion as a rabbi. "Is it against our religion to turn on a radio in a funeral car?"

That problem had never arisen in the sixty-three books of the Talmud. Nor did I have the opportunity to follow my usual practice of consulting an Orthodox authority. I answered weakly:

"As far as I remember, the Talmud lists no restrictions on radio."

We listened, as Joe DiMaggio was robbed of a home-run by a spectacular catch executed by an obscure out-fielder; and the Brooklyn Dodgers mercifully "stayed alive" for one more day.

Generation Gap

In the rather circumscribed world of synagogue life, any reference to "the president" can have only one connotation: the man who presides over the Board of the congregation. That is why my secretary's voice was casual when she informed me that the President's secretary was on the phone.

The voice from the White House startled me. "Rabbi Kertzer, you are planning to be with the President next Friday at out conference on drug abuse. We understand you keep kosher. What would you like for lunch?"

I asked her what was on the menu and she answered, "Fish—probably flounder." I answered her that that was perfectly fine for me. She wondered about the need for kosher plates and I explained that it was no problem.

A few hours later, after Sabbath worship that evening, I mentioned to a few congregants over a cup of tea that President Nixon's secretary had called, and I repeated her words, "We understand that you keep kosher."

There were murmurs of "only in America" and a great deal of excited approval of the President's sensitivity to Jewish dietary concerns.

On Sunday morning, seated around a table with my Confirmation students, all tenth-graders, I recited the story about the White House query, "We understand

that you keep kosher." Tom, sitting opposite me, visibly
paled, and was obviously upset.

"What's wrong? What did I say?"

The rest of the students joined in an agitated chorus,
"Did you hear what the White House secretary said,
rabbi? They've got a file on you."

One of them moved her fingers in an imaginary ges-
ture, as if to pluck a card from a White House print-out
drawer, and read:

"KERTZER—He's kosher."

Tribal Customs

Everyone has experienced the discomfort of a sore throat, with varying degrees of intensity. But this one was different. My throat felt as if a dentist's drill, on which were mounted revolving razorblades, had been plunged into my throat. And I was on the open highway on a long automobile trip, my destination three hundred miles away.

As I passed through the main street of a New England town, located off the super-highway, I noticed an M.D. sign. A solicitous physician explained that there was only one way to get relief.

"Use steam. Lots of steam."

The next morning, in the home of my cousin whom we were visiting, I walked into the kitchen where the maid was preparing breakfast. She was a young Japanese girl, recently arrived from Osaka. I asked her for a towel, but she did not quite grasp what I was saying. My cousin, using gestures, explained that her guest, the rabbi, needed a towel and a kettle of boiling water. The girl watched with interest, as I brought a chair close to the kitchen stove, spread the towel over my head, and breathed in the steam for a half-hour.

The following year, I happened to visit the family again. Uchida had quickly mastered English, and welcomed me graciously. At the morning breakfast table, as she bent over to pour coffee, Uchida whispered:

"Rabbi, aren't you going to say your prayers first?"

"I've already said them."

"Oh, I'm so sorry. I didn't bring you the towel and kettle."

I visualized Uchida's return to Japan. In her lecture to the Women's Club of Osaka, she would describe some of the native customs of America:

"Ladies, let me tell you some of the strange worship practices of the Jewish tribes. Every morning, before breakfast, they take a towel and a kettle of boiling water, and . . ."

Anthropology has fascinated me since my college days, and I have devoured the writings of Frank Boas, Clark Wissler, Margaret Mead and a score of gifted ethnologists. But, sometimes, I wonder if their writings do not occasionally miss the mark. What if one part of the jig-saw puzzle was overlooked?

A friend of mine invited two Navajo chiefs to his home in Phoenix. In the tradition of a good Jewish mother, his wife served chicken soup with matzoh balls. Their guests lavished compliments on their hostess. Would she mind writing out the recipe to bring back to their New Mexico reservation?

It is easy to envision a 21st century study of the Navajos, written by a University of Tel Aviv anthropologist:

"On the first night of Passover, during the Spring of 2067, we sat down to a repast. A Navajo matron smilingly brought out one of their tribal specialties, a steaming bowl of chicken soup with matzoh balls!"

The Ten Tribes:
Lost, Strayed or Stolen

Whatever happened to the lost ten tribes of Israel? Normally, people don't care too much about what happens to lost tribes. The Moabites disappeared, along with the Assyrians, the Babylonians and the Hittites, and I can't think of anyone who is still looking for them. I once heard a young, enthusiastic archeologist lecture on the culture of the ancient Sumerians. With verve and passion, he informed us that over 4,000 years ago the Sumerians had flush toilets! Yet I know of no one who has spent a minute of time trying to locate traces of the Sumerians. On the other hand, people are still searching for the lost ten Tribes of Israel.

I once figured out the reason. Those Israelites had the good fortune of acquiring the label, lost. Most of the peoples of antiquity disappeared. But some historian, perhaps moved by a mischievous impulse, attached the adjective, lost, to the captives of Sargon II, and thus loosed a torrent of speculation that has continued unabated for 2,695 years. 'Lost' can mean, to cease to exist, which is probably what happened to the exiles. Or else it can mean, mislaid, and that is where all the trouble started. We are still searching.

When I visited Tokyo in 1958, I made a pilgrimage to the home of the saintly Kagawa, whom many called, the

Dr. Schweitzer of Asia. Dr. Kagawa had spent his life among the earth's disinherited, risking his health by working in a leper colony, and taking into his home the victims of advanced tuberculosis. When the near-blind Christian saint greeted me in his home, he reacted to the name, Rabbi.

"We Japanese are your brothers. We are of the lost Ten Tribes. Just compare our language with your Hebrew: the vowels and the consonants are the same. So many of our syllables are alike. We are children of Abraham, like you."

Among other nominees for the Lost Ten Tribes are the American Indians. I have never heard any of them lay claim to Hebrew genes, but there have been European explorers who have visited native tribes in Mexico, who have reported that Indian chiefs have greeted them with words that sounded like, *Sholom Aleichem*, the traditional Hebrew phrase for welcome. Tourists returning from Mexico are sure that the tribes of 8th century B.C. Israel found their way to the Americas.

Some branches of the ancient Israelites—Israel was the name of the ten northern tribes—are still alive and well. (Modern Jews are, by and large, descendants of the two surviving tribes of Judea.) The Samaritans, numbering no more than a few hundred, are still to be found in the Holy Land, detached and separated from their Judean brethren, but they retain their Hebrew character today.

And in the depths of Ethiopia live the Falashas, dark-skinned, but lacking any of the Negroid features of their African neighbors. Even the Ethiopians accept the tradition that they are Hebraic in origin. The late emperor, Haile Selassie, bears the title, Lion of Judah. Reading between the lines of the biblical Book of Kings, they believe that the Queen of Sheba (Ethiopia) made a lasting impression on her visit to the court of King Solomon. Out of a brief dalliance came an offspring, Menelik, who was the progenitor of the royal family of Ethiopia. Falashas entertain no doubts that they are part of the unlost Ten Tribes of Israel. They are not part of the Babylonian exile; they were simply Hebrews who moved to East Africa.

Far to the North, there are Britons who are convinced that they are definitely part of the Lost Ten Tribes. The Anglo-Israelites maintain that they are more Hebraic than the Jews. Even their name is proof-positive. The name, British is, of course, derived from the word, Brith, the covenant of Abraham. Members of B'nai Brith may have pretensions that they are "sons of the Covenant," but genetically and philologically, they cannot match the claims of the British-Israel people. To clinch their argument, consider the words, Anglo-Saxon. 'Saxon' is a minor corruption of Isaacson, son of Isaac, who was Jacob. Remember that the Lord called Jacob, Israel.

Not to be outdone by the Indians, the Ethiopians, the Japanese, and, some say, the Afghans, the Irish people boast of a folklore that carries them back to earliest biblical roots, beyond Abraham to Noah. They were Hebrews even before there were any Hebrews, according to some of the oldest Irish legends. A 10th century Irish document, for example, informs us that Noah had a granddaughter whom the Bible neglected to mention. She built her own Ark, at the time of the Flood, which landed on a far-off Irish hill. Another medieval document, even older, offers proof that a descendant of the House of David settled in Ireland, and gave his daughter to the King of Ulster.

An ancient Irish tradition solves one of the mysteries of the Bible. What happened to the great prophet of the Exile, Jeremiah? Written records indicate that he did not follow his fellow-exiles on their long trek to Babylonia. One early church historian wrote that Jeremiah ended his days in Egypt. But no one knows, because the Bible leaves us in doubt.

The Irish have the answer. Legend reports that the prophet Jeremiah was brought to the shores of Eire, and "helped write the laws of Ireland according to the Ten Commandments". Several centuries earlier, a daughter of Pharaoh, disturbed by Moses' rise to power, joined her husband in a flight to Spain, and ultimately to Ireland. The couple carried her dowry, consisting of the stone which served as Jacob's pillow, when he dreamed of a staircase to heaven.

I thought of some of these old legends when I was aboard the U.S.S. *United States* on its record-breaking voyage across the Atlantic. On the high seas, we observed on our starboard side the pride of the British fleet, the *Queen Elizabeth*. She had left port six hours before the American ship, and now we were passing her in mid-ocean. Patrick O'Rourke, who occupied a cabin next to ours, was the loudest in his shouts of triumph, as we swiftly sailed by. Standing on the upper deck, he waved a glass of whiskey in the direction of the hapless Queen. Pat noticed that I did not share his enthusiasm, and he shouted in my direction.

"Come on, rabbi. Let's teach those bloody English a lesson. Both of us can show them a thing or two."

I assumed then that the Irishman's camaraderie was based on his feeling that my attitude was colored by the recent politics of Palestine. The Irish and the Jews both had had trouble with the English. But it has since occurred to me that Patrick was probably steeped in the lore of his Gaelic forebears. One of those ancestors may have been on that other Ark, the one that landed on the west coast of Munster!

According to Irish folk history, the Ark of Noah's granddaughter had a different kind of passenger list than her grandfather's. Jewish Bible records that Noah's guests entered in respectable two-by-two fashion. The Irish Ark contained fifty women and three men!

Cousin Abigail and the Arabs

In July, 1967, a month after Israel's Six-Day War, we visited my cousin Abigail in her Jerusalem home. We had just missed seeing her Sabbath afternoon guests, her pre-1948 Arab Neighbors. She had invited them for afternoon tea, and it was a joyous reunion. They had been friends as well as neighbors. I wondered about Abigail's attitude toward Arabs. She had been a widow since 1936, when her husband, an engineer, was cut down by Arab bullets while he was surveying a road on Mount Carmel.

In her own mind, Cousin Abigail made a clear-cut distinction between the political Arab and the neighborly Arab. The first, was a creature of government; the second, a human being. In all my visits, I had never heard either a word of reproach, or, for that matter, of self-pity.

Abigail's Sabbath guests had included two families: four parents and four teen-aged children. As one mother to another, her Arab friend pointed proudly to her sixteen-year-old son, Ali, and boasted about his keen mind and serious devotion to books.

"Our boy, Ali, will go on to university studies. Now that we are one city, he will be able to enroll in your University—I mean—*our* University. (She was referring to the Hebrew University in Jerusalem. Effortlessly, this

Arab mother had made the transition from the Old City to the New.)

Abigail was not startled by the sudden proprietary posture of her Arab neighbor. My cousin was born in the first decade of the century in Ness Ziona, a town south of Tel Aviv, which her family had founded in the early 1880's. Although it was established by Jews, Arabs flocked there in large numbers to work on the farms, especially in the orange groves, the vineyards, and with the bee-hives. For the first thirty years of her life, Jews and Arabs lived peacefully together in Abigail's town.

The first of my twenty visits to the Holy Land—Palestine, and then, Israel—occurred in 1936. My father had given me the address of my great-uncle Chayim, and my wife and I visited him in Ness Ziona. He was eighty-eight years old, tall, and white-bearded. In the course of our visit, he mentioned that they were awaiting the arrival of his mother-in-law. We thought we had misunderstood him. The mother-in-law of an eighty-eight year old?

The old lady, excited and bursting with energy, arrived in the late afternoon. She had spent the week-end at a wedding-party in a neighboring town. At the age of 114, she had danced with members of the family. This energetic centenarian was introduced as my great-great-aunt who had settled in Palestine fifty-seven years previously, at the age of fifty-seven. She was the widow of the founder of Ness Ziona, Reuben Lehrer.

Our host, Abigail's father, proposed a toast to the visiting American relatives, addressing us in Yiddish:

"May you live till 120!" (Then, turning to his great-aunt, he modified the toast:) "Till the days of the Messiah!"

The lively lady responded: "I guess I will make it till then."

On our next visit to their home, we learned that she had only made it till 116.

Over the years, my awareness of our Ness Ziona family stimulated my interest in the Arab world, as well as it reinforced our family love for Israel. I studied Arabic —even taught it for a time at the University of Iowa— and, as a teacher of comparative religions, I learned a great deal about the Islamic faith.

Our 1936 visit, which I mentioned earlier, coincided with the first major Arab riots. There have been two lesser episodes. The tragedy of the conflict was heightened for me by the knowledge that the vast majority of Palestinian Arabs were like Ali's mother. Their goals in life were the basic objectives of every one: good education for their children so that they could improve their status in life, economic security, and good health.

That summer, my wife and I had a breakfast meeting with one of the saints of the Holy Land, the venerable Henrietta Szold, a Baltimore woman, who had established the Hadassah Hospital. At the age of seventy-seven, Miss Szold maintained a twelve-hour-a-day schedule, from seven to seven, so that our meeting was at six in the morning in Jerusalem's Eden Hotel where she lived.

Henrietta Szold lamented the lack of communication between Arabs and Jews, and wanted her people to take the initiative. She had called on the Jerusalem radio station, operated by the British, to announce in Arabic:

"In the name of Allah, the Compassionate One, in your boycott campaign, please don't keep your children away from our hospitals."

Her concern for Arab children, a large proportion of whom had been blinded by trachoma until they were treated at Hadassah clinics, was all the more amazing to us because we had heard the tragic news of the previous day: Two Hadassah nurses, on their way to treat Arab children, were cut down by Arab assassins with dumdum bullets. Yet, Henrietta Szold still spoke of her dream of Arab-Jewish harmony.

The frustration of those who shared in her dream grew with the years. Like the grandfather of Jordan's King Hussein, Abdullah, thousands of morally sensitive among the Arabs, and many more who simply wanted what Ali's mother sought—health and education and economic well-being—were eliminated by bullet and knife.

Not many miles from Ness Ziona is the city of Gaza, and the area which, today, is called the Gaza Strip. A *New York Times* correspondent reported that more than 1000 Arabs were killed by guerillas because they cooperated with the Israelis. (Nov. 21, 1974) Their crime had been that they climbed aboard trucks to work in fields, like those of Abigail's family,—some of them, undoubtedly, in neighboring Ness Ziona. They, too, were searching for what all human beings wanted, the basic necessities of life.

The *Times* report quoted the Mayor of one of Gaza's towns: He said that his family had been *mukhtars,* or leaders, of the town of 20,000 for three centuries. "The Israelis open all their cities to all our people, they give us work and they give us money.... We have lived under Turkey, England and Egypt, and the Israeli people are better."

It is tragic to contemplate the thought that, if the United Nations had its way, and the Gaza Strip is returned to Egyptian control, the 350,000 inhabitants will revert to their previous status which kept them imprisoned in the small area, *not* permitted to move to Egypt, or even to visit except under special circumstances, in contrast to their free movement into Israel since 1967.

In the summer of that year, a Bethlehem Arab brought
his wife to the Hadassah Hospital in Jerusalem. She had
been informed that she had a terminal disease, involving
her thyroid gland. Her husband had read that, with free
access to Israel, they could take advantage of recent research in that field at the Hadassah Medical Center. The
Arab family was delighted to learn that, indeed, there
had been a research breakthrough, and that, with proper
treatment, the Arab woman's condition was curable.

One of the ancient Hindu religions maintains that all
of life is an illusion. The more I observe the so-called
Arab-Israel conflict, the more intense is my feeling that
so much of it is illusion. Does it really matter to Ali's
mother, or to the Bethlehem husband, what flag flies
over their town? Especially, since that flag did not exist
when they were in their youth?

I visited a farm community on the southern shore of
the Sea of Galilee, and was impressed with the landscape, consisting of thousands of banana plants. Having
recently travelled through the tropics of Panama, I asked
my host how they managed to preserve their plants in
the face of occasional frost. In Panama, banana plants
flourish and are renewed because they never experience
freezing temperature.

Our Israeli host described the devastating snow-storm
of 1950, which not only destroyed their crops, but also
made the planting of a new banana crop impossible.
"Luckily for us, the farmers, over on the other side of
those hills,"—he pointed across the Jordanian border—
"offered to replace them so that we could begin afresh."

The Israeli farmer expressed no surprise at the generous action of the Arabs across the border. The fraternity
of farmers knew no artificial boundaries made by man.
Their enemies were the frost and the marauding insect
and the rain-less skies. Their concern, with God's
bounty, not with man's blindness.

Somehow, the idea persists in my mind that Abigail's grandchildren and their neighbor, Ali, will ultimately discover their common humanity, and the mutuality of their goals in life, and will greet one another with *Sholom* and *Salaam* in the land that gave mankind its first vision of Peace.

Cousin Abigail and the Cossacks

For cousin Abigail, Hebrew has always been the language of piety. Most of her seventy-two years were spent in pre-Israel Palestine, but, despite her intense devotion to the new State, the Hebrew tongue, for Abigail, is the lingual instrument of the Bible and the prayer-book. Naturally, when she served as principal of an Orthodox girls' school in Jerusalem, she must have utilized modern idiom: the Bible and the Talmud had no words for astrophysics or zoology. But when Abigail wrote to me to deplore my tardiness in answering her letters, she would conjure up the vocabulary of Jeremiah: "What iniquity hast thou found in me, cousin Morris, that thou hast removed thyself far from me?"

Early in June, 1975, I sat at her dinner-table in Jerusalem, sipping tea at meal's end. Abigail glanced furtively at her watch, and with studied casualness, wondered if I would like to watch Israeli television.

"Why not?"

"It's exactly nine o'clock!" She leaped from the dining-room table toward the set.

The international basketball tournament was being played in Yugoslavia, and tonight was the night of judgment: Israel versus the Soviet Union!

I had heard snatches of a previous game. Israel had

outplayed their arch-enemy, Poland. What rejoicing
there was in the gates of Jerusalem! Old scores had been
settled. Painful memories of ghetto tyrannies were still
fresh for many Israelis who had escaped from Warsaw,
Lodz and Cracow.

But tonight was *the* Night. Israel's finest five, recent
victors over Rumania, was now pitted against Russia's
basketball stars. And wonder of wonders, Communist
Yugoslavia, forsaking political prejudices, had expedited
the telecasting of the game to the Israeli network while
it was being played.

Israel's team was first on the floor, and there was an
organized cheer from the stands: "Yis—ro—el, Yis—ro
—el—Rah—rah— rah!"

Abigail beamed as she explained that the Yugoslavs
had no love for the Russians.

Five giants poured on to the floor, tall, broad-beamed
gladiators from the Soviet Union, towering over the Israelis, both in height and in width. Abigail launched into
a dirge, a wailing which lasted till half-time: "The ways
of Zion do mourn; she findeth no rest, for all her persecu-
tors overtake her."

The Israeli center gazed up at his gargantuan rival as
they prepared to jump. Abigail shouted at her television
set:

"Behold there cometh up the champion, the Philistine
of Gath, Goliath by name!" Right out of the Book of
Samuel.

Eisner passed to Berkowitz and set up a perfect shot
for Brodie under the basket, but the long arms and
fingers of a Russian easily blocked the arching ball. Abigail fumed in frustration:

"Pogromtchik! Cossack! Enemy of Israel!"

As the Russian lead lengthened, Eisner slid under the
outstretched palms of his opponent and the ball fell in

for two points. Abigail's rejoicing knew no bounds.

"The Lord is nigh unto all who call upon Him—to all who call upon Him in truth."

For the next half-hour, Abigail oscillated between quotations from the Book of Lamentations—"How doth the adversaries of Zion prosper"—the Russians scored often—and halleluyahs from the Book of Psalms: "The Lord upholdeth all who falleth, and raiseth up all who are bowed down."

A foul was called on Yannai, yielding the Russians another three points. Abigail shook her fist at the Yugoslav referee:

"Antisemites!" She turned to me: "What more can you expect from a Communist referee?"

Only a few minutes remained before half-time. Abigail, ever the teacher, added a new word to my vocabulary, *hafsakah*, intermission or, break.

Eisner, Berkowitz and Brodie were fleet-footed, but they raced up and down the court with little reward for their efforts.

Abigail raised a cry which I did not understand: *"Pesek. Pe—sek!"* I had never heard the word before. It finally dawned on me. Abigail was urging her weary Davids to take *pesek*, time out—in the face of Goliath's onslaughts.

At *hafsakah*, half-time intermission, I left cousin Abigail glued to the television set. The Union of Soviet Socialist Republics led by fourteen points. It was a handicap which even Abigail's invocation of divine mercy could not overcome. Somehow I lacked the courage to remain with her till the final moment of reckoning. Prime Minister Rabin was scheduled to leave on the morrow on a critical mission to Washington. Four terrorists had been discovered on the Lebanese border. Rockets had landed just north of Haifa. All this travail Abigail could take in her stride. But for the pride and joy of Israel, the invincible heroes of Jerusalem and Tel Aviv, to suffer humiliation at the hands of the Cossacks was more than the human spirit could endure.

"How hath the Lord covered the daughter of Zion with a cloud of His anger,

And cast down from heaven unto the earth the beauty of Israel."

You Can Trust Your Doctor?

Can a mountain talk? No. But, sometimes, a hill can tell a story, especially if it is a Judean hill. The prophet, Isaiah, declared that "the mountains and the hills break forth in song." They certainly might be able to carry a tale.

Not long before the renowned Doctor Bernhard Zondek of Jerusalem died, I was invited by one of his American colleagues to a dinner party in his honor. My wife and I mentioned to him that we had met in 1936, in the city of Jerusalem, during our first visit to the Holy Land. Even at that time, Dr. Zondek had gained a world-wide reputation for his research in problems of fertility and sterility. Among other achievements, the gynecologist had developed the Aschlein-Zondek test for pregnancy: what the medical authorities call "the original endocrine tests, from which all others have stemmed." He and his two brothers had been forced out of Nazi Germany. The three Zondeks, all brilliant medical researchers, were Hitler's gifts to the emerging state of Israel.

At the dinner table, my wife described our first bus-ride from Tel Aviv to Jerusalem. We recalled the hazardous hair-pin curved roads of the early days. What a hair-raising experience it was in those days before Israeli engineers eliminated the curves!

Dr. Zondek was amused at our reference to the highway approaching Jerusalem.

"Those Judean hills remind me of a patient I had, a number of years ago. An old lady came into my office in Jerusalem. She had just arrived on the bus from Tel Aviv.

" 'Doctor,' she said in Yiddish, "my physician in Tel Aviv told me that I need a hysterectomy. So, I took the bus to see you."

"I examined her, and expressed my agreement with her own doctor. "Yoh, bobeh! . . . Yes, grandma, you really need a hysterectomy."

"She responded with a half-whispered, *'ich ll zehn* . . . I will see'!

"I repeated again, this time a little more vigorously, that she needed surgery. Once more, the same response, as if speaking to herself: 'I will see."

"I tried to overcome her hesitation with a reference to my medical credentials. (His list of honors covers pages in Who's Who.)

"She still insisted: "I will see.'

" 'I just don't understand you, my dear. Here, you just travelled from Tel Aviv to Jerusalem, over all those dangerous curves. You put your life in the hands of a young bus driver. Can't you do the same for me?'

" 'Ah, Doctor Zondek, that's different. He went *with* me!' "

Moscow Miracle

David Ben Gurion once said that a student of Jewish history who does not believe in miracles is no realist. The full impact of that paradox was not brought home to me until I witnessed the current rebirth of Russian Jewry.

In 1956, I organized a delegation of rabbis, one of the first of its kind, to visit the Soviet Union. When we returned, I wrote a series of articles for the *New York Times*, the last of which underscored the hopelessness of the fight against "all the machinery of state, the educational institutions, the mass media, the arts and literature of the Communist regime." Our delegation returned with the conviction that "there was little question as to the ultimate victory" of the totalitarian State. I was prepared, in 1956, to join the historians in writing off the three million Jews of the Soviet Union, as a lost community.

First of all, there was terror. We felt that we were visiting a vast prison-house. The shadow of the executioner was gone—since the death of Stalin—but we could see, in the eyes of every Russian Jew whom we met, a pervasive sense of fear: fear that some one would report their mere proximity to American visitors; fear that they would join a brother or sister in Siberia because the taboo word, Israel, had been dropped in our conversation.

Then, there was frustration. We sat with Chief Rabbi Schlieffer around a table in his Moscow office. Could we rabbis of America send his congregation prayerbooks, for we saw so few in the hands of the old worshippers? His answer: "We need no prayerbooks. Look at all the prayerbooks here." And he pointed to a table that was bare. For a moment, we were puzzled. How could an empty table be full of prayerbooks? Then, we noticed the rabbi's two "assistants", seated on either side of him, taking notes. They were not his assistants, but agents of the Commissar of Cults who was in charge of minority religions within the Soviet Union.

Our frustration was compounded when we visited Commisar Prychodkov, Director of the Council of Cults. Would we be permitted to mail prayerbooks to the Moscow Synagogue?

"Of course," he reassured us. "This is a free country. Jews, and every one else, have freedom of worship. You can send all the prayerbooks you want. . . . but . . . , on one condition: if the Chief Rabbi requests them.' "

We hinted that such a request was not likely to come. Commissar Prychodkov blandly remarked: "That is the kind of rabbi we have here in Moscow."

Our most trying problem was of communication. When we entered a synagogue, we were immediately escorted to seats of honor on the pulpit, far removed from the congregants. All our protests were unavailing. Placed next to us, were officials of the Synagogue, who whispered to us, during the services, about the glories of Communist freedom.

One of my colleagues, Rabbi Israel Mowshowitz, whose fluency in Russian would have enabled him to speak to individuals without the intervention of our guide, Alexei, kept imploring our Russian shepherd to arrange a game of chess. At the breakfast table, each morning, the rabbi would go through the same routine: Alexei promised a chess partner, and the rabbi complained that he was a fanatic about the game. After four days of apologetic postponement, the rabbi warned Alexei that another day without chess would disturb his nervous system. "You can't keep putting me off."

That same afternoon, Alexei blithely announced that he had scheduled a chess game for Dr. Mowshowitz— with another American tourist who had made the same request.

Finally, we were overcome with a feeling of hopelessness about the future. No more than a handful of rabbis, who were aged and decrepit, for three million Jews! Without a seminary for young religious leaders, how could the Jewish faith survive? Forbidden to promulgate the elements of the faith and the Hebrew language used in prayer; or to teach anyone under eighteen; who would instill Jewish consciousness in the next generation?

The one glimmer of hope appeared in an unexpected place: the Moscow Conservatory of Music. Jan Peerce, the world-renowned tenor, had invited us to attend his concert, part of a cultural exchange program. The audience, of well over one thousand, was both young and Jewish. They greeted his French, Italian and German songs warmly. His Russian selections were enthusiastically applauded. Then, the Metropolitan opera star returned for three encores—without introduction or explanation . . . His three Yiddish melodies seemed familiar to his audience. Peerce's last number was the plaintive cry of a Hasidic rabbi, arguing with his Maker: "O Lord, what do You have against Your own people, Israel? All peoples have a home. Why not we?"

The walls of the auditorium shook as the youthful

crowd stamped their feet, rose and cheered for several minutes. All of us wept, including Jan Peerce. Without a word being spoken, these young Jews were saying that the Kremlin's victory over the souls was not a total one.

Eighteen years have passed. I would have guessed that, by the 1970's, there would hardly be a trace of Jewish resolution left. Yet, young ballet dancers, like the Panovs, have left their native land—a country which pours its adulation on the ballet in a way I have not witnessed anywhere in the world—to settle in Israel, in a frontier nation that, despite its ambitious musical institutions, has not yet organized a ballet company. And, in Russia, countless Jewish scientists, physicians and engineers, without a trace of affiliation with a synagogue of communal organization, have risked dismissal, humiliation and constant harassment, in order to identify themselves with their ancestral heritage.

David Ben Gurion must have been thinking not only of modern Israel, but of these brands plucked from the fire, in totalitarian Russia, when he maintained that a historian who does not believe in miracles is not a realist.

The last day I was in the Soviet Union, an unexpected visitor came to see me in Leningrad. I had sent word to his daughter through a synagogue worshipper. A few weeks earlier, four people came to see me in my New York City office. They were of my parents' generation. As a matter of fact, the two brothers and two sisters had known my parents, a half-century ago. They had left their brother in Russia, but were certain he was dead. Since the devastating Battle of Leningrad, during World War II, they had not heard from him. They gave me his daughter's address; perhaps, she was alive. His brothers had been "saying *Kaddish*"—the memorial prayer—for many years.

As the old man approached my table in the Dining

Room of the Europa Hotel, he eyed me suspiciously. Could I possibly be an *agent provacateur?* I introduced myself as a son of his childhood classmate, David Kertzer. He remembered my father, but still retained his reserve. From my jacket pocket, I plucked out a snapshot which his family had given me. There he stood, fifty years younger, with his two brothers and two sisters. He burst into tears, and held the photograph to his heart.

A few days later, I met with his family in Newark, New Jersey, and reported my experience.

"You can stop saying *Kaddish* for your brother."

I have stopped saying *Kaddish* for my fellow-Jews in Russia.